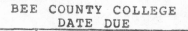

T.E.Lawrence

T.E.Lawrence

Peter Brent

Introduction by Elizabeth Longford

G.P. Putnam's Sons. New York

First American Edition 1975

© George Weidenfeld and Nicolson Limited
and Book Club Associates 1975

House editor Jenny Ashby
Art editor Sandra Shafee
Layout by Juanita Grout

Printed in England

SBN: 399–11584–6
Library of Congress Catalog Card Number: 74–32436

Contents

Introduction

WAR IS A NOTORIOUS SEED-BED OF LEGENDS. A war-hero who has used in his lifetime three different names and could have used a fourth – T. E. Lawrence, 'Ross', 'Shaw' and Chapman – might seem to be conducting a legendary search for either identity or anonymity. But in fact the legendary element of Thomas Edward Lawrence was originally focused upon his war-record as 'Lawrence of Arabia'. It was his fabulous exploit in raising the Arab Revolt against Turkey during World War I which first kindled the popular flame. Lowell Thomas's lectures after the War, followed in 1926 by the publication of Lawrence's own masterly *Seven Pillars of Wisdom*, completed his canonization.

Then came doubts. Accidentally killed in 1935, this blue-eyed, clean-limbed patriot soon appeared to be anything but a plaster saint. Some mysterious crisis had smitten him in Deraa when he was tortured by Nahi Bey. But what? And for the last twelve years of his life he had been flagellated at intervals by a friend. But why?

With subtlety and entirely without dogmatism Peter Brent has explored many possible interpretations of the Lawrence enigma. At times the narrative moves as swiftly as one of Lawrence's own racing camels. Speed, excitement and suspense are the essence of the capture of Akaba and the destruction of Turkish railway-lines. At other times Peter Brent reins in the story and falls into step with the psychologists, as when he points out that Lawrence's extreme shyness was balanced by a habit of 'waving and hallooing' like a child who demands attention. Again, Lawrence's wearing of Arab clothes could be either a tawdry love for fancy-dress or an attempt to discover his own identity by sinking himself in an alien culture and rejecting his native mores.

In any case, why did this gifted human being need to resort to such subterfuges? After all, he had a first-class mind, an imagination which gave him the freedom of classical archaeology and twelfth-century Syria and Palestine, remarkable powers of endurance, an amiable father and a mother who worked in the mission field. His parents, however, were not married and the father's real name was Chapman.

The effect on the son of his illegitimacy is brilliantly analysed by Peter Brent and seen as the probable matrix of his self-disgust. To the son, 'Lawrence', 'Ross' and 'Shaw' were all equally creatures of fiction, while Chapman was fact. The ambiguity spread even to his birthday, which his father gave as 15 August 1888, his mother as 16 August. (Lawrence chose the 15th – the same as Napoleon.) To him, the love which had procreated him was lust, passion was sin and asceticism and devotion to a cause the only safety. Yet, having reached this purified nadir, Lawrence's actual experiences turned the whole edifice upside down. His devotion to the Arab cause brought it only betrayal; his suffering in the Bey's torture-chamber brought him, not strengthened asceticism, but perverted pleasure. It was the 'Old Adam' in us all – the 'Old Man', as the Baptismal Service puts it. And so, pretending that an elderly relative (the 'Old Man') required him to be beaten, Lawrence persuaded his friend to lay on.

I once saw T. E. Lawrence near the end of his life. As 'Aircrafts-man Shaw' he had arrived on his motor-cycle at Lady Astor's home, Cliveden, for tea. He looked like a child who has gone prematurely grey in spirit though not physically. Peter Brent aptly quotes Churchill's remark about him: 'He is a fine animal, but he cannot live in captivity.' True; though Lawrence's captivity was imposed on himself by himself. Today his tragedy is no less significant than it was forty years ago. For hindsight shows that it was acted out against a Middle Eastern problem as intractable yet as deeply human as his own.

Elizabeth Longford

1 Preparations for an Unknown Mission

I have given them a topic of conversation for
a week – *Deux cent cinquante kilomètres,
Ah la-la, qu'il est merveilleux.*

To his mother from Mont St Michel, 26 August 1907

I got on to the Kala'at into a lonely place and
lay down on my back from about 8 till 2.30,
feeling most weak and ill. At about 3 I sat up and
tried to dress, but fainted promptly for about an
hour, and again then when I made a second
try. . . . About 5 p.m. I got to the village after a
very hard walk.

Syrian travel diary, 29 July 1911

T E. LAWRENCE WAS ILLEGITIMATE. One begins with this fact,
so much less startling in our day than it was in the eighties of
the last century, because it was from it that so many of the contradictions and enigmas in Lawrence's character almost certainly
stemmed. He was born in Tremadoc, in Wales, on 16 August 1888,
given the Christian names of Thomas Edward and the surname his
father had adopted, Lawrence. The father's actual family had been
the Chapmans, land-owners from County Meath in Ireland, one
name in the long and aristocratic roster of the Anglo-Irish
Ascendancy. His wife had, according to some accounts, been able
to combine a sour disposition with a passionate temperament, the
former saddling her with the nicknames 'Vinegar Queen' and
'Holy Viper', the latter with a penchant for adultery (though this
last charge may malign her). After the birth of four daughters had
failed to temper her character, Thomas Chapman eventually
eloped with, classically, the children's governess. He seems to
have chosen his new name of Lawrence at random, and to have
lived thereafter a somewhat nomadic life, during which he never
allowed lack of money or the change in his circumstances to inhibit
his established inclinations. As an aristocrat, he avoided books,
regular work and the handling of money, retaining his self-respect
by proficiency with gun and rod, at the tiller, in the saddle and
over a bottle. Distantly, Raleigh featured among his ancestors; a
little more recently, Henry Vansittart of the Hellfire Club. He was
easy-going, good-humoured and altogether fitted for the baronetcy
he inherited (though in a name he had long forsaken) during the
watershed year of 1914.

The pleasant contours of this Edwardian character, however,
are almost hidden from us by the formidable angularity of the
mother's personality. It was she who dominated the household
and, in one way or another, the five boys who were born of this
unexpectedly romantic association. Yet about her too there flow
the ambiguities and uncertainties which make Lawrence's story so
hard to clarify: was her name Sarah Maden or Sarah Junner? Was
she illegitimate and her father Norwegian, or was she Scottish and
the daughter of a Sunderland shipwright? What is confirmed is
that she was zealously religious, profoundly puritanical, an
economical manager, largely self-educated, proud, sometimes
harsh and narrow but always admirable in her strength and almost
bitter steadfastness. Throughout his life, no one seems ever to
have usurped her place in T. E. Lawrence's private pantheon or
even for a moment to have cushioned him from the effects of her

12

formidable personality. As to what she thought of him, it is plain from the list she later set down of his boyhood accomplishments that she regarded him with a sort of tough, yet matter-of-fact, pride. He seems at times to have astonished her – she says that he 'learned the alphabet without a single lesson from hearing his elder brother taught' and that later, 'any book he took up he seemed to read at a glance, but he knew it all, as I soon found out. No tree', she adds, 'was too high for him to climb and I never knew him to have a fall.'

This was while the family lived in the New Forest, having already trekked from Wales to Scotland, from Scotland to the Isle of Man and from there to France. In September 1896, when Ned, as the family called him, was eight years old, they moved on to Oxford, partly in order to allow the boys, until then taught at home, to go usefully to school. It was then, therefore, at the City School for Boys, that Lawrence began what he would later dub 'an irrelevant and time-wasting nuisance', his period as a day-pupil. Their Indian file of cycles in strict order of the boys' seniority, Ned thus in the second place, all as though in uniform, hooped by the blue and white stripes of their identical jerseys, the Lawrence brothers became a familiar sight on the roads between their home and the school.

Perhaps a little eccentrically for an English schoolboy, Lawrence preferred what a friend would later call 'his archaeological rummagings' to the regimented enthusiasms of team games, or the simple hierarchies of sporting competition. The sports he enjoyed – gymnastics, cycling, cross-country runs, paper-chases – were solitary, competitive only in that they involved the overcoming of inert forces and demanding of stamina and a sort of self-searching courage. Archaeology provided him with artifacts which made tangible a past which at times almost obsessed him. He arranged that any pottery fragments found by labourers working on the foundations of some of Oxford's new buildings should be put aside for him; these, his mother records, he assembled with the aid of plasticine, recreating with an enthusiast's reverence bowls and jugs used by the citizens of that place centuries before. With his bicycle to give him the freedom of the countryside, he ranged across it, a precociously erudite raider bringing home a booty of brass-rubbings with which to festoon his bedroom.

Those calm, elongated knights, stretched in their watchful images, were the inhabitants of his preferred world – the twelfth century was its period, the Crusades its most compelling activity,

FAR LEFT Krak des Chevaliers, one of the Crusader castles that Lawrence visited during his Middle Eastern tour while still a student. The Crusades and Crusader castles were to form the subject of a special thesis.

LEFT This painting of Lawrence as a boy on the beach is by M. S. Tuke and now hangs at Clouds Hill, Lawrence's home from 1923.

Carcassonne: Lawrence explored some of the French medieval castles on a cycling tour with his father in the summer of 1907.

the Crusaders' fortifications its admired architecture. As a younger child he had orchestrated war games on the theme of breached walls and conquest; now he made the keeps and towers beneath which genuine warriors had clashed in iron-clad heroics his primary interest. In large note-books he kept details of portcullis and counter-scarp, of battlement or kitchen-flue, taking careful photographs to supplement his jotted texts, then clambering on his machine to pedal home again, or on to where yet another tattered or resplendent barbican stood unrelenting against the centuries.

Meanwhile, he read, and, if neither as omnivorously nor as voraciously as his later claims suggested, it is clear that throughout his years as schoolboy and student he digested a large number and a great variety of works. It was through books that he felt the first influences of the Middle East, reading Sir Henry Layard's volumes on his excavations at Nineveh, and later, when he was an undergraduate, Charles Doughty's classic account of desert travel, *Arabia Deserta*, a book of which the style as much as the vision it expressed was to affect him profoundly. Yet in a way, all these were only surrogates, echoes of some inner dream, not yet clearly defined, perhaps, but already pressing, which only action and achievement would, he must have thought, ever satisfy. Once one of his schoolfellows in the Lower Fourth discovered gleefully that he was a day older than Lawrence; Lawrence gravely commiserated with him because he had not been born, as Lawrence himself had, on Napoleon's birthday. Such schoolboy vainglory is not, of course, unusual, but it has in Lawrence, a man perhaps justly accused of never having grown beyond his early teens, a greater significance than it might have in some others. One senses in his interest in heroes, in his assiduous pursuit of a violent and romanticized past, in his determinedly solitary sports and hobbies, in the proclamatory nature of his aloofness, a character which not only was inherently different from that of others, but which was determined to make as much of this difference as possible.

When Lawrence was sixteen, he fell awkwardly and perhaps fatefully during a playground struggle. He told his family that he had been going to the aid of a smaller and bullied boy, an action certainly in line with the quixotic ideals of twelfth-century chivalry. The consequence, however, was a broken leg, the pain of which he bore without a murmur – drawing on that fortitude many would in later years remark on. It was only after an hour or so of the gentle tedium of a mathematics lesson that his brothers

16

discovered what had happened and wheeled him home on a bicycle. 'He never grew much after that,' his mother was to write later, and it is true that in all his photographs he gives an impression of smallness, possibly exaggerated by the slightly disproportionate length of his head from forehead to jaw. It is not certain now how tall Lawrence actually was, estimates varying from an implicitly accepted maximum of 5 feet 6 inches to some three inches less; in the autumn of 1914 he apparently tried to enlist but was turned down because of his lack of height. Now and again he refers to his size with some bitterness and one can imagine that this abrupt cessation of growth in a boy who until then had been large for his age may have had unsuspected effects on his character. The reticence and uncertainty which seem to have shadowed some aspects of his personality will in any case not have been lightened by this new set-back; the difference he had always felt between himself and those about him had been increased.

It was shortly after this that, for his own especial use, a bungalow at the bottom of the garden was rebuilt and redecorated, a strangely lordly present for a boy still in his mid-teens. One suspects that he now needed a little distance between himself and his parents, as though the very closeness of the family, once protective, had become in some ways menacing. It is a fact that he became from this time on more unpredictable in his behaviour, more eccentric in the hours that he kept; his mother always insisted that he was never out after midnight, but his friends tell other stories, including tales of icy swims on mid-winter nights, and when Lawrence decided to study history in his last year at school, his visits to his coach, L. C. Jane, tended to begin at midnight. (Although the teacher's own hours must have been somewhat eccentric, especially as Lawrence sometimes did not leave until four in the morning.) In some of these exploits there may be detected an element of posturing, a selfconsciousness of attitude. This is not unusual in adolescence, but one wonders what role Lawrence saw himself as playing, how he hoped to be considered by his contemporaries. What cannot be doubted is that he already saw himself as in some way extraordinary and that he took great pains to be deflatingly proficient at those activities, such as photography or cycling or pistol-shooting, which he so energetically pursued.

Surrounded by his growing library, his brass-rubbings, his fragments of ancient pottery, and perhaps already under the gaze of his famous bronze head of Hypnos, the bringer of sleep,

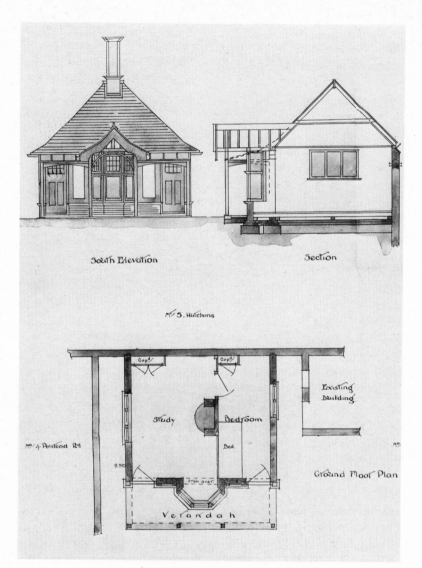

South Elevation

Section

Mʳˢ S. Hutchins

Study

Bedroom

Cupᵈ

Cupᵈ

Existing Building

Nᵒ 4 Polstead Rd

Bed.

8 PO.

Arch over

Verandah

Ground Floor Plan

Nᵒ

A plan of Lawrence's bungalow in the garden of his parents' Oxford home. His mother claimed that it was built for him as a study, but Robert Graves wrote: 'To avoid surveillance he refused to sleep in the house at all, but used a summerhouse in the garden (he built it himself) as his bedroom.'

Lawrence seems somewhat self-indulgently to have idled away much of his time, day-dreaming and relaxed, as though the evidence of his book-heavy shelves and recondite ornaments was enough to place him among Oxford's languid élite. Reverie and optimism modified reality – he was to insist, for example, whether as one of his endless practical jokes or because truth and fiction had become interchangeable, that his bronze Hypnos, actually an easily available copy, was genuinely Greek and had been discovered by him on an Italian rubbish heap. Since he owned the head in 1910,

18

at which time he had never set foot in Italy, this story seems unlikely; perhaps it was the rubbish heap which travelled to him, rather than he to the rubbish heap. He was to receive a salutary shock, however, for although he had helped by winning scholarships to pay his own school fees, when in June 1906 he sat for a history scholarship at St John's College, he failed comprehensively.

That summer, however, he was cycling enthusiastically through the heat and poplar-shadow of France, tracking down twelfth-century castles with the same determination which had already transfixed most of those in England and Wales like granite butterflies in the collecting cabinets of his note-books. His letters home are full of erudite observation – 'I will not bother you with details,' he writes to his mother from Dinard, 'except to remark that the mail collar of the knight, just above the tabard, is excellent.' From Guincamp ten days later he describes the *château* – 'It is nearly a trapezium in plan, that is an irregular polygonal figure,' such schoolboy pedantry reinforced by the jargon of the specialist – 'The door stands in the centre of a sort of demi-lune or rabelin. . . .' Indeed, the letters seem more the disquisitions of a scholarly guide than the remarks of a boy to his mother, although it is plain that he is showing off, and happy to do so. According to his companion, his schoolfriend C. F. C. Beeson (nicknamed 'Scroggs'), 'Lawrence's main preoccupation was with the minds of the designers of these defensive works. . . . He talked little of campaigns and military art in general.'

On a flat, sea-hammered beach Lawrence found an equal satisfaction in hurling himself on what he called the speed-trials of his new cycle, bending over the dropped handle-bars, his legs desperately pumping, the Atlantic wind full behind him, Scroggs perhaps crouched beside a marker, watch in hand, his eyes on the convulsed and straining figure of his friend. 'I rode a measured half-kilo. on the sand in 40 seconds exactly,' Lawrence wrote home, adding with some justification that he thought '30 miles per hour was distinctly good.' Soon, however, he was back to his main concern, describing *châteaux* and castles – 'On the 1st floor there was also a latrine, not worthy of special mention' – having meanwhile dismissed almost in an aside his poor showing in the scholarship examinations: 'The result is on the whole not as good as I had hoped. . . . In the Divinity I had hoped for more. Polit. Econ. is not surprising; I expect we both made asses of ourselves.' His *insouciance* does not entirely convince; on the

19

other hand he had taken first place in the English examination and thus had grounds for optimism. There would be, he pointed out, another chance the following year.

It was during this tour that he first came across Ruskin, buying a copy of *The Stones of Venice* and so joining that legion of aesthetes and art-lovers whose passion had been both defined and given substance in Ruskin's edged and careful paragraphs. As with many who are inwardly tormented, Lawrence found the great abstractions, Nature and Art, easier to respond to than he did the complexity of human beings. If Layard's *Nineveh and its Remains* had brought him images of an ancient Mesopotamia which would obsess him and in the end decide his destiny, Ruskin's style would lend him cadences later to be discerned, alongside those transmuted from Doughty's more applicable *Arabia Deserta*, in his own monumental *Seven Pillars of Wisdom*.

During that autumn, Lawrence worked with his tutor, toiling through the calm Oxford nights towards his goal. In February 1907 he wiped out his earlier rejection, his Welsh birth helping him to a place in that traditionally Cymric college, Jesus. And it was to Wales he now travelled, cycling alone this time, sending from Carmarthen and Chepstow and Caerphilly another cascade of architectural minutiae with which to dazzle his parents and his brothers; there is hardly a line in these letters where the perplexities of personality are allowed to peep from behind this shield of erudition. One finds few signs of intimacy or affection – he might have been writing to some favoured teacher, or the parent of a schoolfriend. There is to my eye a deadness in what he writes, a coldness, a clinging to observation and abstraction, which might have sent a shiver of misgiving down any parent's back.

And indeed crisis was to strike in that very year. Was it, as some biographers have claimed, because he was told then about his illegitimacy? The moment was perhaps right, with Lawrence poised on the threshold of university and thus of manhood. Yet he confided to close friends that he had been about ten years old when his father had told him the truth. Nevertheless, his actions now, and his reticence about those actions, seem inexplicable unless one considers them the result of something at least as serious as the discovery that his parents were unmarried. It is of course not impossible that he was told the facts while still too young to understand them, but that now in the hurly-burly of adolescence he had his attention drawn to them again, to react this time with an intemperate revulsion.

20

Most people seem to have assumed that it was his shame and his disgust at the fact of his bastardy which so disturbed him. I wonder, however, whether even in 1904 his reaction would have been so extreme if that had been the full extent of his shock. The family was after all a real one, close-knit, apparently affectionate and with strong bonds between the brothers. It seems to me that Lawrence's deeply ingrained guilt had other, though connected, causes. In some ways his situation was not dissimilar to that of the young Byron, privately debauched by a nursemaid who publicly professed an adamantine puritanism. In the same way, Lawrence's mother faced him with the contradiction between her private conduct and her public protestations. Just as Byron, over-perceptive and precocious, could rarely thereafter reconcile the physical and the emotional, particularly in his relations with women, so Lawrence (perhaps compensating too for lack of height as Byron did for lameness) seems all his life to have eschewed sexuality, and certainly heterosexuality, altogether. Once he knew the circumstances of his and his brothers' birth, it is unthinkable that Lawrence did not have great difficulty in matching the harsh religiosity of his mother with the inescapable fact that she had borne five sons out of wedlock and that to do so she had run off with another woman's husband. Despite all her insistence on morality, he could hardly help seeing her as the sexual being she must in fact have been. Yet sex, he had been taught through her own puritanical precepts, was shameful and dirty, and although he later achieved a fairly free and relaxed attitude to many sexual matters, it is likely that during that period of his life those precepts, whatever he thought of them, loomed large. The conflict between the dirt of sex and the purity of his mother, between the dirt of maternal sexuality and the purity of maternal precept, may well have become intolerable to an adolescent. One can believe that such thoughts and images would rise to torture him as only flight might allay.

In any case, whatever the reason, he fled. In a rehearsal for the later pilgrimages of his self-disgust, he ran to hide himself in the anonymous ranks of the army. He joined the Royal Artillery, but it is not clear how long he remained there. Some people have suggested it was only for a few weeks, but in May 1929 he apparently told Liddell Hart, then working on his biography, that he joined the Artillery 'about 1906 . . . and did eight months before being bought out'. Significantly, asked to amplify this later, he replied, 'This is hush-hush. I should not have told you. I ran away

A view of the High, Oxford,
in the 1900s, when Lawrence
was a student. Queen's
College and All Souls are
on the right, and University
College on the left.

22

from home' – and here a row of dots marks missing words – 'and served for six months.' He was, he said, frightened by the other soldiers' weekend roughness, but in any case wanted the whole episode kept out of print.

He himself wrote for Liddell Hart's use the final version of this incident: 'In his teens he took a sudden turn for military experience at the urge of some private difficulty. . . .' One is forced to wonder at his coyness, even when one allows for his normal secretiveness, selective though that was. It was clearly something close to the core of his being which forced him to uproot himself in this way, to bury himself among the boisterous illiterates and semi-criminals of the Edwardian army. His despair passed, however, or at least he came to terms with it. In due course his father, pointing out Lawrence's youth (he was in fact still under age), was able to buy him out. Quietly he returned home, saying nothing about where he had been, and behaving as though he had passed these weeks on some tour of Britain's castles more protracted than usual; it was a long time before even his brothers had any idea of what had really happened.

That summer of 1907 he travelled to France again, cycling this time with his father, as enthusiastic a cyclist and photographer as Lawrence himself. Once more a cascade of architectural detail came grittily tumbling from his letters; by August, however, he was alone and in the South for the first time. His tone is more relaxed now – 'had 15 miles of up and down to St Somebody-I-don't-want-to-meet-again, and then a rush down 4000 feet to the Rhone' – yet can be swiftly reined back to permit a glimpse of the young sensitive face-to-face with Nature:

I was looking from the edge of the precipice down to the valley far over the plain, watching the green changing into brown, & the brown into a grey line far away on the horizon, when suddenly the sun leaped from behind a cloud, & a sort of silver shiver passed over the grey: then I understood, & instinctively burst out with a cry of *'Thalassa, Thalassa'* [in Greek characters in the original] that echoed down the valley, & startled an eagle from the opposite hill. . . .

At this point, however, something appears which one can often find in Lawrence – a kind of deflating and self-deprecating humour; he goes on, 'It also startled two French tourists who came rushing up hoping to find another of those disgusting murders their papers make such a fuss about I suppose. They were disappointed when they heard it was "only the Mediterranean"!'

24

In the same letter he writes again of that warm and ancient sea — 'I felt that at last I had reached the way to the South, and all the glorious East; Greece, Carthage, Egypt, Tyre, Syria, Italy, Spain, Sicily, Crete . . . they were all there, and all within reach . . . of me.' Hindsight provokes one to see something prophetic in this exultant catalogue, but the fact is that it is the standard reaction of imaginative northern youth to the seductive South. Lawrence, who later claimed to have been obsessed all his life with the dream of bringing liberty to Asia, to have wanted since childhood to be the centre of a national movement, seems in fact at this stage to have become a fairly standard example of an imaginative, educated young man. Certainly he felt himself to be different from those around him, but so with some justice do all imaginative and intelligent people. He dreamed of doing great things, but if one does not have such ambitions at nineteen, one will never develop them; alas, there is no corollary that if one does have them, they will be fulfilled!

He was a proficient photographer, an energetic cyclist, an accurate shot; he had a detailed knowledge of medieval castles, having collected these as other youths might have postage stamps or memories of football; he had a knowledge of archaeology, was fairly fluent in French, had a grasp of the classics; in his speciality, twelfth-century history, he was able and even at times impressive. His personality was both forceful and elusive, and he had quirks which emphasized this aloofness — he hated, for example, to be touched, and would go to some lengths to avoid physical contacts. He was a mixture of potentialities and contradictions, of accomplishments and expectations — he was, in short, typical of that sizeable echelon of young men who year by year arrive at the universities with at least the possibility in them of doing great things and who, if they do them, are taken later to have shown early signs of genius, but if they do not, are never considered anything remarkable. There is nothing so selective as the hindsight of biographers.

Anarchic, eccentric, self-driven — for such a man, university made a more attractive stage than had school. He retained his bungalow, however, which allowed him more freedom than did his room in college. He read with continued voracity, though his later claim that he had during his Oxford youth read all the fifty thousand books in the Oxford Union Library, as well as numerous other volumes, seems on the face of it unlikely. (It depends on what he meant by 'read', for the term may have included the

25

skimming and skipping of the accomplished browser; otherwise even at the rate of ten books a day, every day, the task would have taken him some fourteen years! He did eventually concede, however, that he had avoided the Union's large collection of theological works.) He made nocturnal trips; explored an underground stream, a trip which he and his friend E. F. Hall were the first to make, but which later became quite popular with canoeists in search of a new sensation; climbed in the normally adventurous manner the façades and pinnacles of the ancient colleges; during the summer of 1908 he traversed once again his now-beloved South, travelling almost to the shadow of the Pyrenees, examining the fortress walls of Carcassonne, the architecture of Narbonne, of Albi, of Toulouse.

But, as he wrote with telegraphic concision to Robert Graves, 'At Jesus read history, officially: actually spent nearly three years reading Provençal poetry, and Medieval French *chansons de geste*.' There is, of course, something self-advertising in this proclamation of an erudite idleness, but there is no need to regard it with too much scepticism; Sir Ernest Barker, who knew the family from before 1905, has testified that Lawrence's younger brother Willy also had a passion for the poetry of those southern troubadours. In any case, 'When time came for degree, wasn't prepared for exam.' But in August 1908 he had written to his mother that he had visited 'Niort which was magnificent; nothing could possibly have been more opportune or more interesting for my thesis.' So it was already as early as his second year at the university that he was preparing to submit a special thesis to supplement the normal papers. Obviously its subject would be based on his particular speciality – the Crusades and the Crusader castles. By the summer of 1909, he had, in Sir Ernest Barker's words, 'determined, as a good scholar would, that he must go and see the castles for himself' and so to make a Middle Eastern tour – though perhaps a 'good scholar' would not have felt the need for a supplementary thesis with which to impress his examiners.

A consequence of this decision was that it led to his friendship with the Arabic scholar D. G. Hogarth, who was at that time keeper of the Ashmolean. (Lawrence may have met him earlier, for he told Liddell Hart that he attracted Hogarth's attention while still a schoolboy by the way he assisted in the arrangement of medieval pottery in the Ashmolean's cabinets; certainly he had haunted those galleries over the previous five years.) Hogarth, a small, trim man, was from then on to hover over Lawrence's life

A photograph taken in 1899, showing the interior of the Ashmolean Museum. Even as a boy, Lawrence spent much time here pursuing his passion for medieval pottery.

a little like a genie, leaning benevolently down at intervals in order to reduce an obstacle here, set a new course there or, at another place, provide some succulent opportunity. Hogarth, a member of that zealously imperialist group the Round Table, may have imbued Lawrence with some of its notions of Anglo-Saxon supremacy, its mistrust of French and German policies and its advocacy of the Commonwealth ideal. It was information about Syria and Palestine that Lawrence wanted now, however, and perhaps an introduction to Hogarth's friend Charles Doughty, whose cadenced descriptions of the desert still sang in Lawrence's memory. Hogarth tried to warn him off the Middle East – in summer Syria was hot, it was at all times expensive since guides and servants were essential, and the Turkish government had to provide an *Irade*, a sort of visa or licence, in order to establish a traveller's right to be in the country at all. Doughty proved equally unenthusiastic: 'In July and August', he wrote, 'the heat is very severe and day and night, even at the altitude of Damascus . . . it is a land of squalor where a European can find evil refreshment.'

Lawrence, however, was not only obstinate, he took a positive pleasure in subjecting his body to the utmost of natural rigours. When still in the Officers' Training Corps he had side-stepped an order forbidding cadets to sleep out by keeping only his legs inside his tent 'and his head among the guy ropes', as E. F. Hall wrote later. Talk of the hardship that faced him, therefore, proved bait rather than dissuasion; later he would claim that he had deliberately been training himself 'for a great endeavour', but the truth is that he could not help himself. He searched out opportunities to test himself, to overcome privation and pain. He expressed himself neither in prose nor in action so much as in endurance. Physical suffering meant more to him than any other sensation, but it would be many years yet before the complex springs of this fascination would be revealed to him.

Nothing, therefore, could prevent him from setting sail in the P & O liner *Mongolia*, the necessary documents in his pocket, his means and equipment slender, but his expectations high. It was his intention to walk through the Middle Eastern summer. Such fears as he might have had were alleviated when in Beirut he learned that the teachers at the famous American College there spent their vacations in precisely the kind of raffish promenade he had planned. Carrying a spare shirt, a camera and tripod, and a Mauser pistol for protection, he set off southward along the sea, swung eastward at Sidon and thus, as he wrote to his mother from

Safed, 'walked inland to Nabatiyeh, & from there to Banias, & from there here in about a week'. By the beginning of August he was back in Beirut, '& therefore the first part of my work out here is finished'. For the moment, so was he, for he had contracted fever, but he wrote home at great length, describing the food he had eaten, the people he had seen, the houses they lived in, much of it in precise, almost pedantic detail. For once the real and present world had almost nudged his beloved castles off the page, although he had visited all those on his itinerary.

Next he marched northward, through Lebanese Tripoli and Latakia, finding his way in the process to the castle at Safita – 'a *Norman keep, with* ORIGINAL *battlements* : the like is not in Europe : such a find' – as well as many others: 'my Thesis is I *think assured*,' he wrote exultantly. He was attacked by a lone and elderly marauder on a horse, whom he sent packing – 'when I . . . plumped a bullet somewhere over his nut he made off like a steeple-chaser . . .' – before finally reaching Aleppo. From there he had intended to travel on to Damascus, but it was now near the end of September, he was intermittently ill, his feet were badly blistered and his boots worn out and, worst of all, his money had come to an end.

He wrote to Sir John Rhys, the Principal of Jesus College, to explain his prolonged absence: 'I have perhaps, living as an Arab with the Arabs, got a better insight into the daily life of the people than those who travel with caravan and dragoman. Some 37 out of the 50 odd castles were on my proposed route and I have seen all but one of them. . . . My excuse for outstaying my leave must be that I have had the delay of four attacks of malaria when I had only reckoned on two. . . .' Again that curious mixture of apology and bravado; but the malaria was real enough, nor was it his first brush with that disease, for he had already caught it from what were then the vast and voracious swarms of mosquitoes in the Camargue. The intermittent fevers of this disease were to afflict him for the rest of his life.

Sir Ernest Barker remembered later that at the end of one of his lectures in October 1909, 'a man came up to me whom I did not recognize – a man with a very fine face, which seemed thinned to the bone by privation'. Thus Lawrence had been altered by the rigours of his first contact with Syria and Palestine, countries later to be the stage upon which he would enact the flamboyant central drama of his life, countries which were to create and recreate and finally, perhaps, destroy him. But even as an undergraduate

Safita, looking west to the Mediterranean. The Norman keep rises
from one of the twin hills on which the city was originally built.

31

he was dreaming of the great book which he would write – a not uncommon dream, perhaps, among the literate young – and now he knew what its title would be: *Seven Pillars of Wisdom*, a work which he would print himself about seven Middle Eastern cities. Fine print already obsessed him, and he had brought back with him vessels of crushed murex, that unassuming shellfish from the juices of whose body Tyrian purple is made, to dye the vellum of the work he contemplated.

In the meantime, other and perhaps less congenial work awaited him. He faced his final examinations, for which he knew himself less than thoroughly prepared. He had, however, his thesis with which to dazzle his examiners. There were some five months left for him to do the work, but it is claimed that he wrote the fifty-page essay in three days and nights, presumably because in June 1911, as he wrote to his brother Will, 'I left my special subject (the Crusades) till the last two weeks of term. It was mostly done while the examination was still in progress in three all-night sittings: Special subjects, if you know all but the facts, are a matter of simple cram.' This comes as part of a passage of advice about his brother's university courses, and continues, 'I should certainly not recommend doing it (except to know your ground, if it is territorial) before the last term: or the term before last, leaving the last for revision . . . always read something that throws a side-light on the set authorities . . . ,' all of which suggests to me, as it did to Richard Aldington, that he meant by this his preparations for the examinations themselves and not the writing of his thesis.

The Military Architecture of the Crusades has not been accepted by even his greatest admirers as among his better works; it argued that those who had built the Crusader castles of Syria and Palestine had brought their techniques with them from Europe. In this it set itself against the accepted view that the Crusaders had in fact learned from the sophisticated methods of Byzantium, bringing their new knowledge with them when they returned to their homelands. One suspects that there was the usual element of bombast in this choice of viewpoint, as well as a residue of his childhood-long love-affair with the twelfth century, its knights, architects and poets. In any event, despite the impolite surprise of most later commentators, Lawrence's work was sufficiently vigorous and well-enough researched for the examiners to overlook whatever scholastic defects it might otherwise have suffered from and grant him a First Class degree.

Thus equipped by education, experience and fortune, he finally left Oxford. He may have had the idea of writing another thesis, this time on medieval pottery. In any case, that summer he was again whirling down the roads of France, dragging his plume of white dust behind him as he searched and scavenged in its history. But by the end of the year he was once more on his way eastward. Hogarth had for the first time reached into his life: he had arranged a demyship at Magdalen College for him, thus assuring him as a scholar there of £100 a year, and at the same time engaged him at a small salary as his assistant in the excavations he was about to begin at Carchemish, a tempting mound beside the Euphrates, not far from Aleppo. The two incomes between them would make it possible for Lawrence to do what he most enjoyed, in the one part of the world where he most wanted to be.

His first experience of winter in the Middle East was not encouraging, however – snow lay on the mountain passes, Hogarth when he arrived could not reach Aleppo because the railway lay under thirty feet of drifts in places. The party travelled south to Haifa, then overland to Damascus; grey winter parted for them when they reached Deraa, where a southern sun shone at last. Later the place would make its own shadows for Lawrence, but now he travelled with anticipation towards the elongated mound at Carchemish, hoping perhaps to uncover in himself too the hidden treasures he sensed lay within.

It is likely that there now began the only period of uncomplicated happiness in Lawrence's life. It is not that he had forgotten his ambitions; far from it. But the work that faced him was not so arduous that its difficulty undermined its interest; he was far away from the order and the underlying ambiguities of his home; he was in a place where his own idiosyncrasies had been overtaken by the oddity of being European, a lot he shared with his British companions; he was young enough to dream of future triumphs and may have seen himself as on the first approach-road to them; his situation offered him the chance of travel as well as the opportunity to exercise his pedantic but oddly unequal erudition; the rigours of the country and the climate challenged his passion for endurance, for suffering – and above all, he was . . . one is tempted to say 'in love'; certainly he had, as it were, fallen into a deep state of friendship.

I think it is clear from his subsequent history that Lawrence was always out of touch with some of the deepest springs of his own feelings. He was a man who presented himself to the world in the

33

Archaeological Experience at Carchemish

Lawrence's appointment to Carchemish was to have far-reaching effects. Not only was he able to indulge his consuming interest in the classical past; he also became strongly identified with the Arab cause, through his friendship with Dahoum.

Together with Leonard Woolley, he produced a report on the excavations at Dyerabis, which were carried out for the British Museum. These photographs are from Woolley's and Lawrence's report: BELOW Stone relief of two soldiers. RIGHT Excavation in progress.

guise he chose; all other contacts and connections he avoided. Released by distance from the demands and conventions which had hitherto hemmed him in, living during a period when the unconscious pressures of the psyche had not yet been widely recognized, it was perhaps the case that emotions he might not otherwise have allowed to show now rose to the surface and demanded expression. It has been claimed categorically that Lawrence was not a homosexual and I am certainly in no position to deny this. What remains true is that he demonstrated in his later writings a tolerance for homosexuality he never displayed for heterosexual relations, or indeed for women other than such surrogate mothers as Bernard Shaw's wife, Charlotte. (He fatuously told Graves that he had not had much to do with girls in his youth, and that the habit had stuck.)

It seems likely that had he been a sexual person at all, Lawrence would have preferred men as his partners, that physical contact between males seemed to him to have a rightness – what he called 'cleanness' – which sexual relations between men and women did not. But Lawrence was not a sexual person; he did not like to be touched, he avoided familiarities, when finally he did feel the need to relieve his tensions physically (and those tensions not perhaps sexual at all) he did so without any of the loving contact between bodies which for most people can alleviate their human loneliness by the sudden poetry of passion. He was, perhaps, an ascetic, one who lived by the medieval ideal of abstinence; on the other hand, he may have been a man maimed, wracked by a vicarious guilt and incapable for these or hormonal reasons of physical love.

In Carchemish, however, he found Dahoum. He was a local boy, some fourteen years old, bright-eyed, slim, beautiful. He was fair-skinned, enough so for Arab love of paradox to have named him *dahoum*, 'darkness', although his real name was, not Sheikh Ahmed as has for so long been thought, but as Knightley and Simpson reveal in *The Secret Lives of Lawrence of Arabia*, Salim Ahmed. Lawrence took to him almost at once, taught him to read and write, taught him photography, made him his assistant, later brought him into his house. The house itself signalled their affection for each other, for on the roof crouched a nude carving of Dahoum, Lawrence's own work and difficult to understand as other than a public proclamation of his feelings.

In the summer of 1911 he set off on one of his pedestrian treks, his companion for at least part of the time young Dahoum. Alone,

OPPOSITE Dahoum photographed by Lawrence. He was a donkey-boy or water-boy at Carchemish.

36

however, he caught dysentery, he suffered pain from an abcessed tooth and he finally stumbled into Jerablus, the village which lay in the shadow of the Carchemish mound, at the point of collapse. There he found shelter in the house of his other great friend among the Arabs, the foreman Hamoudi. He was tall, thin, but very strong, bearded and, according to his own statements, the killer of some six or seven men. Now, however, he nursed Lawrence, despite the rumbling discontent of the Turkish authorities, who wanted no dead Englishmen to account for and demanded Lawrence's ejection. Soon it became clear even to Lawrence that he would have to accept the fact that he was seriously ill; early in August he arrived by carriage in Aleppo, and a few weeks later, wracked by dysentery and malaria, he reached his home in Oxford. 'But don't imagine I am ill,' he wrote to his long-time friend V. W. Richards: 'merely a hopeless weakness that sits me down after a hundred yards is done on foot, and also I cannot go upstairs save crab-wise.'

By the end of the year, however, he was once more in the Middle East. The Carchemish dig had been threatened by shortage of funds, but Hogarth had been able to reinforce these. First, perhaps to learn more about the basics of archaeology, Lawrence spent some time with Sir Flinders Petrie, the Egyptologist, near Cairo. He seems not to have been happy there, and his letters take on a slightly defensive, jeering tone – 'the Professor is the great man of the camp . . . he is a man of ideas and systems, from the right way to dig a temple to the only way to clean one's teeth. Also he only is right in all things. . . .' Early in 1912 he was back again, established in Carchemish, and welcoming his new colleague, Hogarth's successor, Leonard Woolley, young then, not yet distinguished nor rewarded with a knighthood.

Woolley has described Lawrence with a cool, though quite affectionate, accuracy. He tells of Lawrence's dislike of ridicule – 'probably due in part to his knowing that other people found it hard to take him seriously. It was hard. Physically small, with a head disproportionately large, very unobtrusive with his quiet voice and tendency to long silences . . . he was not on the surface of things impressive. . . .' Woolley remarks on his 'fondness for "dressing up"' and describes his blazer of French grey trimmed with pink and the 'gaudy Arab belt with swinging tassels' with which his white shorts were held up. Such a belt was worn only by bachelors 'and Lawrence had his tassels made bigger than anyone else's'. Woolley comments on the fact that Lawrence personally

Lawrence photographed
by Dahoum and wearing
his clothes.

A view of Aleppo: a quiet
courtyard off the bazaar.
When the British Museum
closed down the Carchemish
expedition temporarily,
Lawrence travelled on foot
to Aleppo, keeping a record
of his route in his diary.

41

Lawrence (left) and Leonard Woolley on the excavation site.

liked very few Arabs, although he 'was already an enthusiast for Arabs as a whole'; he also remarked on the friendship between Lawrence and Dahoum – 'a boy of about fifteen, not particularly intelligent . . . but beautifully built and remarkably handsome' – but says that Lawrence 'knew quite well what the Arabs said about himself and Dahoum and so far from resenting it was amused . . .'. He cites as an example of Lawrence's dislike of being ridiculed – a common failing in those given to playing practical jokes – an occasion when a clamorous bunch of Kurdish girls mobbed him and almost stripped him in their boisterous curiosity: 'He could not take it as a joke, and would never go that way again. . . .' It did not occur to Woolley that in this single incident Lawrence had run headlong into all his phobias at once.

Lawrence, and to a lesser extent Woolley himself at this point, seem not to have taken the business of archaeology too seriously, although Woolley mentions Lawrence's extraordinary visual memory, which would allow him to fit a newly discovered fragment to some other particle of pottery dug up perhaps months before, 'and although there were many hundreds of such in our store-room he was always right'. But, Woolley says, 'I had not the insight to see then the genius that was in him, though I could recognize that he was unusually gifted and remarkably lovable; but I was quite conscious that closely as we lived together I did not know him really well.'

Lawrence at this time was still living in dreams as much as in the landscape; indeed, he was to do so for several years yet, one feels. It was a world created by Doughty, by the songs of chivalry, distantly by the Bible, observed through the sensibilities of a Ruskin and now given a new and romantic dimension by James Elroy Flecker, the poet, whom Lawrence had met in Beirut. This period in Lawrence's life, therefore, brought fantasy into phase with reality in a way which could not help being deeply satisfying. He saw himself, so many have suspected, as the Doughty of a new generation, and his demanding tours on foot may be considered not only another stage in his self-punishing, self-testing search for hardship, but also an attempt to build a platform of experience from which to launch himself upon the world as this century's poet of Arabia, comparable with the Burtons and Doughtys who had preceded him.

There were, according to both Lawrence and Woolley, occasional brushes with the Turkish authorities, with a team of German archaeologists working not far away, with Kurdish tribesmen. In

Sir Flinders Petrie arranging
some of the pottery he found
in southern Palestine, at an
exhibition of ancient pottery
and bronze work held at
University College, London.
Lawrence was sent to him in
Egypt in 1912 to learn
up-to-date methods of
excavation, recording
and preservation.

45

some of these, the young British scholars behaved with a simple, near-military arrogance in tune with the imperialist certainties of their times. Held up in their work by the local Turkish governor, who said that no permits for them to dig at Carchemish had been received, Hogarth's documents not being transferable to Woolley, Woolley got his way at revolver point. During another dispute, a court case, all their papers were seized by the authorities, where-upon Woolley held the judge under his pistol, the camp's cook, apparently a two-gun chef, kept the spectators quiet, while in the next room Lawrence forced the governor to hand back the documents. More happily, they circumvented a Turkish order restricting their building programme to a single four-walled house by making it U-shaped, giving themselves some half-dozen rooms and a courtyard to look out on.

In 1913, Lawrence's younger brother Will arrived to visit him, on his way to teach in India. Ned, he wrote home, was 'a great lord in this place'; he was 'known by everyone, and their enthusiasm over him is quite amusing'. Not everyone was always so enthusiastic; Hubert Young, later knighted and distinguished but then a lieutenant also on his way to India, records the reaction of a Kurd who had been challenged by Lawrence after illegally dynamiting fish. Brusquely pointing out the crime, Lawrence had told the man, 'Now pick up thy fish, tie them in a bundle and come with me to the police station!' Not all the 'lesser breeds without the law' were equally amenable to such an approach. The Kurd stared down at this diminutive Englishman. 'What is this?' he asked: 'Who art thou? I know thee not. I know not thy father nor yet thy mother. I gather up no fish. I tie them in no bundle. More-over, I come not with thee to the police station.' Lawrence would have forced the issue, but one of the man's companions drew a knife, a stone was thrown, bloodshed was imminent and the British withdrew. He reported them to the local Turkish police inspector, threatening to see that the offical was dismissed if they were not arrested. 'Tell me what I should do with them, *effendi*?' the inspector is reported as asking. 'Flog them,' said Lawrence, stamping off. There is something less than attractive in Lawrence's calling in the authority he himself had so often flouted to finish what he had begun, yet something typical also of his worthier characteristics in the bland courage with which he had tackled the Kurds in the first place – and something as well, perhaps, of the Anglo-Irish land-owning blood in his veins in the detestation with which he regarded the dynamiting of fish.

OPPOSITE Leonard Woolley, who was later to acquire a solid reputation for his work in archaeology. He had a high opinion of Lawrence's abilities, especially in handling the Arab workmen, from whom he doubtless picked up his knowledge of various dialects.

46

Despite these skirmishes, or perhaps partly because of the spice they added to the life, Lawrence always considered his Carchemish years as the happiest of his life. During them, he discovered a landscape and a people by which he would, for a while, be increasingly bewitched. Whether he travelled as widely and as far as he later suggested may be doubtful, but he did travel, and suffer for his travelling, and learn through it. During these journeys he may also have kept an eye on Ottoman doings for Hogarth, a man renowned for being a mine of unexpected information on the Turks, who, during World War I, emerged from his apparent scholarly obscurity to direct the Arab Bureau in Cairo. At one time, in 1912, Lawrence may have been forcibly recruited into the Turkish army, to escape only after three desperate weeks; at another time, he claimed, he laboured for a while as a stevedore. Like many men who vaguely feel themselves a misfit, he seems to have been tempted to, as it were, disappear, to identify himself with another people, another culture, a different and more attractive way of life. He knew, of course, that it could not be done, and was in any case too European, too steeped in Oxford, too ambitious, to allow himself thus to disappear from his own world.

He was always a man fascinated by the effect he had on others. There was certainly until 1918 a theatricality about him which demanded an audience. The stories he told about himself bludgeoned his listeners with a sort of vainglorious modesty, a throw-away boastfulness – and were not always, in the event, strictly true. One gets the sense that he was a man searching for approval. But who would have been in that ideal audience whose applause would once and for all have stilled his self-doubts? Is it his mother whose praise he wanted? Or was it, then and throughout his life, those shadowy relations of his who were never to acknowledge him, his father's family, the Chapmans? Would not their acceptance of him have permitted him peace, a certain place in the world, an identity shadowed by no doubts?

There are hints from time to time during his life that this may have been the case, but whatever the reason there is no doubt that for all his diffidence, his almost aggressive shyness, he spent much of his life waving and hallooing, like a child demanding to be noticed. In 1913 he brought Hamoudi and Dahoum to Oxford – whatever the generosity of this, was it not also a gesture, a snippet from the scenario of some half-written melodrama, the idealized story of the life he might be living, might yet live? Surrounded by his acolytes, the Young Master returns from the East – how

48

gratified he must have been as his two Arab friends, robed and mounted on ladies' cycles, circled again and again the traffic policeman in Carfax or spent hours of bemused admiration over the glazed tiles of public lavatories. And this strain in him, uncontrollable, both desperate and meretricious, has certainly helped to undermine his posthumous reputation, and may even have helped to undermine his self-respect in the years after the World War.

But the years were turning; 1913 flicked away, 1914 slid into its appointed place. Unknown to the actors, a new drama was about to take the stage, and for those who paid attention, the first strains of the overture could already be heard, its discordant notes sweeping across Europe. In that play, Lawrence too would at last be assigned a part, handed his costume and given his cue to perform; the role would be small, but the costume dazzling, his performance charismatic and his fame destructively abrupt. When it was over, it would have overwhelmed him and sickened him of the stage for ever.

2
The Active Bystander

It's very dull: but of course I haven't any training as a field officer, and I don't know that I want to go fighting up to Constantinople. It would be bad form, I think. . . . The Canal is still holding out, and we are forgetting all about it. Turkey, if she is wise, will raid it from time to time, & annoy the garrison there, which is huge & lumbersome. . . . So it's quite easy to run down & chuck a bomb at it, & run away again without being caught.

To D. G. Hogarth, from Cairo, 20 April 1915

THE OTTOMAN EMPIRE, ramshackle but durable, regarded with a natural suspicion British and French activities in the Middle East and resented in particular the British hold on Egypt, once under its own control. Lord Kitchener, in 1914 the British Resident in Egypt and thus its *de facto* ruler, had already realized that in any war which might arise out of the strains and pressures then buffeting the world, Turkey would side with Britain's enemies. Such a decision would leave the Suez Canal uncomfortably vulnerable, because its natural line of defence (as recent conflicts have demonstrated) lay in the Sinai peninsula. In the event of war, British forces would have to be moved into it to protect the canal, a proposal which made maps of the area essential to them.

Sinai, however, still lay under Turkish control, and any map-making there by the British would have to be done circumspectly. Captain S. F. Newcombe of the Royal Engineers was therefore ordered to make such a survey, under the pretext of searching for the route taken by the Children of Israel during their forty-year expedition through the wilderness. Since a scholar of some sort had to be in the party to lend credence to its cover story, and since it would be useful if he knew something of the conditions, Woolley was chosen as Newcombe's companion. Learning that

PREVIOUS PAGES A rock-cut cistern at Wadi Deira. From Woolley's and Lawrence's official report on the Sinai survey, *The Wilderness of Zin*.

An inscription in Greek, found at Beersheba. From *The Wilderness of Zin*.

52

the survey would take three months at least, and not having so much time to spare, Woolley asked that a colleague should accompany him, to take over when the time came for him to return to his normal responsibilities.

It was in this way that Lawrence and Woolley, now under the aegis of the Palestine Exploration Fund, Dahoum faithfully at their side, came to set out to *rendezvous* with Newcombe in Beersheba. Throughout January 1914 they rode and tramped, surveying and considering the ruins they came across, before Woolley separated from Lawrence early in February. Later that month Lawrence

Byzantine capitals found at Beersheba. From *The Wilderness of Zin*.

53

joined Newcombe in Akaba, to discover that the increasingly suspicious Turks had decided to forbid any further work by the expedition, a prohibition Kitchener in Cairo had diplomatically to endorse. Lawrence, however, had set his sights on examining ruins on a nearby island. Although the Turks tried to stop him and, according to his own story, arrested a boatman he had hired, he managed to cross to the island by using zinc tanks as floats. 'I puffed a zinc tank full of air,' he wrote to a friend at the time, a herculean feat which sounds like a *post facto* embellishment of the kind usual with him; he could never resist decorating facts, however bizarre they were, as though he had to force admiration from people – or perhaps as though he wanted to be disbelieved. In any case, he found the ruins 'uninteresting', returned, was thereupon followed by a detachment of soldiers and had, if what he wrote was true, an arduous complexity of turns and climbs and doubles before he could give these observers the slip. But he added, 'We had luck, since we found the two great cross-roads through the hills of Arabah, that serve modern raiding parties entering the Sinai, and which served the Israelites a bit earlier.'

When the survey was over, the greater part of the desolation which is Sinai, and the area north and north-west of Akaba (which would see Lawrence again) had been mapped. Little of archaeological interest had been discovered; the military value of what had been done would on the whole turn out to be greater. Woolley and Lawrence returned to Carchemish, where, as Lawrence described in a letter to James Elroy Flecker, they became involved in a struggle between Kurdish workmen and their German employers. There was a shooting and a death, bullets narrowly missing both Englishmen, blood-money demanded and, after Woolley's intervention, finally paid ('Rössler boggled a bit, but consented in the end'). The dead man was valued at £80. The letter detailing all this was written from England, for Lawrence had now returned, perhaps in order to work on the Sinai survey's official report, a short book of just over 150 pages entitled *The Wilderness of Zin*, intended to appear in order to set at rest Turkish suspicions about that ambivalent expedition. In any case, digging at Carchemish was over for the year – for that year and for the following five, although Lawrence did not know that when the site was closed in June. 'I expect to be another two or three weeks yet in England, & thereafter Eastward,' he wrote to Flecker in that month, but it would be December before he travelled again, and then it would be in uniform.

OPPOSITE Two more illustrations from *The Wilderness of Zin*: ABOVE A Roman blockhouse at Nagb el Safa. BELOW A church at Esbeita, a ruined Byzantine town.

54

The ruins of an old wall at Ascalon. From *The Wilderness of Zin*.

There is a certain mystery about Lawrence's actions and intentions during the first months of the war. Apparently he worked on *The Wilderness of Zin* with Woolley and finished it early in the autumn. In a note on the typescript of Liddell Hart's book about him he noted, 'Woolley and I wrote to Newcombe, when the book was finished, and asked his advice about a war job. . . . Newcombe told Cox, of the Intelligence, about us, and got our names on the

Captain Newcombe dressed
in Arab robes. In fact
Lawrence was only one of
the many Europeans to
adopt the Arab costume for
practical reasons.

waiting list. Woolley lost heart, waiting, and wangled a Commission in the Artillery.' Through Hogarth he was introduced to the
General Staff Geographical Section, where Colonel Hedley, the
head of the Section, was desperately trying to prepare maps of
the Sinai when one by one his officers were being posted to France.
'Nugent hurriedly instructed me,' wrote Lawrence of the last of
these; then 'Hedley and I were left alone in the office.'

Yet he wrote to Robert Graves (to help him with his book), 'Owing glut recruits unable enlist' and there is a note made by Liddell Hart after a conversation with Lawrence (in August 1933): 'T.E. spoke to Hogarth, said he was too small to be taken. Hogarth suggested the Geographical Section. . . .' Hedley himself confirmed that Lawrence had told him he was too small to be accepted by the Army, but makes no mention of the interview's having been arranged by Hogarth. 'He had on some grey flannels and wore no hat. He looked about 18. I said I would get him a commission and take him into my office. . . . He was very efficient and could I think have worked all through the night and hardly noticed what time it was.' The assumption is that Lawrence attempted to enlist, but was turned down and so tried some other route into the Forces; he may, however, have taken his rejection for granted, knowing what the height standards were, for in a series of written answers to Liddell Hart's questions he wrote categorically, 'I did not try to enlist. For the first few months of the war I was working on our Sinai book, and then went to the War Office to do the Sinai map. . . .' There, 'my chief was Colonel Hedley (now Sir – and retired) and he put me into uniform without medical examination or formality.' What is certain is that the Army List for the last two months of 1914 records Lawrence's appointment as 'Temp. 2nd Lieut.-Interpreter' – an announcement in this cartographical context mysterious in itself.

The actual date of this commission was 23 October; only a few days later, the Allies declared war on Turkey and all Lawrence's experience since his first voyage to Syria was suddenly at a premium. He was almost at once made a member of an Intelligence unit to be based on Cairo, one in which he would find himself among a number of people he already knew. Newcombe was one of these, brought back from France for the purpose, Woolley was after all shifted from the Artillery, Gertrude Bell, famous for her well publicized travels, who had been among the pre-war visitors to Carchemish, was added to the team later, as was Lawrence's patient patron, Hogarth. Colonel Clayton, who would be closely associated with Lawrence's activities, and Ronald Storrs, who would become Lawrence's friend (the former later to become a general and the latter a knight), also arrived in Cairo around the beginning of 1915. So did George Lloyd, later Lord Lloyd but then an MP, as was yet another of these Turkish and Middle Eastern experts, Aubrey Herbert. This collection of military men and scholars, travellers and administrators, many of them brilliant

OPPOSITE Lawrence wearing Arab headdress with his army uniform.

58

59

Sir Ronald Storrs, the
Oriental Secretary to the
British Residency in Cairo
and subsequently Governor
of Jerusalem. This cultured
and gifted young diplomat,
who was well versed in
Middle Eastern affairs, stood
by Lawrence throughout.

and several notably eccentric, provided the nucleus for the later Arab Bureau, which would wield an extraordinary influence in the decisions and strategies of the various Middle Eastern campaigns.

It is clear from Lawrence's letters at this time that he was wildly excited to be within reach of exclusive and often secret information, to be breathing an atmosphere heavy with all the incense of power and diplomacy. Treaties, alliances, strategies, conspiracies

Gertrude Bell, the well-known and widely travelled Orientalist who was one of the Intelligence unit at Cairo. She was first introduced to the Middle East in the 1890s when her uncle was ambassador in Persia, and she has left behind evocative accounts of Syria and Mesopotamia. In later years she wrote of Lawrence: 'He lit so many fires in cold rooms.'

– his head was whirling with them. Nor was their fundamental objective always the winning of the war and the freeing of Turkey's unhappy subjects. He considered the activities of the French, both actual and potential, as great a danger to British interests as were those of the Germans and the Turks. He was not alone in these suspicions, and there seems a high probability that Colonel Brémond, the French representative in the area, was as doubtful about the British as they were about the French. The whole area between the Persian Gulf and Damascus, however, was both enigmatic and volatile – one feels that any alliance, any rivalry, was possible, that decisions were reached through the improbable balancing of inscrutable ambitions and that only the oppressive, centuries-old clutch of the Ottoman Empire persuaded those Arab leaders who did so to enter into an alliance with the British and French. It is hard not to believe, glancing at the years which followed, that from their own point of view, all their suspicion was justified and their reluctance too lightly put aside.

There were at this time throughout the Arabian territories several secret societies intent on the overthrow of Turkish hegemony, the most important of which were the Fetah and the Ahab. Among those most deeply involved in these conspiracies was Hussein, Grand Sherif of Mecca. He was the head of one section of the Hashemite family (its name derives from that of Hashem, the uncle of Mohammed) and he was therefore a direct descendant of the Prophet, as all the rulers of Mecca had been since the seventh century. His spiritual authority was enormous and as a result, when Muslim Turkey decided to raise the Arabs against the British and the French by calling a *jehad* or holy war, his cooperation became essential. Hussein, however, considered a holy war on behalf of Christian Germany illogical and certainly had no desire to help the Turks to victory, but was not yet ready for open revolt. He sent his third son, Feisal, to Damascus to confer with the Turkish authorities. At the same time, he gave him instructions to make secret contacts with the Syrian nationalists, while sending his eldest son, Ali, to try to raise an army in the Medina area, and his second son, Abdullah, to Cairo. Hussein himself had before the war asked for British support against the Turks, only to find Kitchener anxious to commit no breach of neutrality; now, with neutrality a distant memory, he felt his chances were rather brighter.

While all this was going on, the British, with Commonwealth troops prominent in their command, had been attempting

OPPOSITE Lawrence with Commander Hogarth (centre) and Colonel, later General, Dawnay (right). Lawrence probably first encountered Hogarth as Keeper of the Ashmolean; in wartime he became the Director of the Arab Bureau in Cairo, set up in February 1916. Dawnay was one of the Bureau's officers.

63

Hussein, Grand Sherif of Mecca, with his attendants. Bent on war with the Turks in the interests of Arab unity, he later proclaimed himself 'King of the Arab Countries'.

unsuccessfully to smash their way through the Dardanelles. (On 20 January 1915, Winston Churchill, perhaps not for the first time, had suggested a landing at Alexandretta, a sea-port on Turkey's Asiatic coast, as a diversion and perhaps even an alternative for the Dardanelles expedition; in March of that year Lawrence had outlined a similar plan in a recklessly uncensored letter to Hogarth and after the war claimed in a note to Liddell

Hart that the scheme had been 'from beginning to end, my invention, put forward necessarily through my chiefs'. He may have thought so, but the idea had been discussed even before the war, and a cable suggesting it again had been sent from Cairo by the Commander-in-Chief in Egypt, General Maxwell, before Lawrence had even left London.) As long as the Dardanelles campaign was their most important commitment against the Turks, the British

ABOVE Emir Feisal's bodyguard, painted by James McBey.

OPPOSITE A portrait of Feisal by Augustus John. Lawrence was
impressed by his 'tall, pillar-like' appearance and dignity.

were not eager to embark on new adventures in dubious alliance with the secret societies of Arabia. After its repulse, however, they tried a new assault by way of Mesopotamia, an effort which was to end in the disaster of Townshend's surrender at Kut-el-Amara in April 1916. The propaganda value of this defeat was increased tenfold when the British offered the Turks £2 million and forty guns to let their army retreat on parole, an offer the Turks rejected with the maximum publicity.

Lawrence had the opportunity to see something of this *débâcle* from close at hand. He had spent the previous year indulging his whimsical eccentricity, always that of a schoolboy thumbing his nose at a conventional world, to the outrage of many of his more orthodox fellow-officers. He dressed untidily at best, and often in pointedly bizarre fashion; he had an airy way of ignoring salutes; he was arrogant and diffident by turns, impudent, out as always to disconcert the lumpish and able as always to keep the friendship of the ablest and most imaginative. He drew maps, he interrogated Turkish prisoners, he learned what he could of those parts of the Arab world he had not yet visited (an area which, after all, included almost the whole of the Arabian peninsula). More importantly, he played a significant role in building up an intelligence network throughout the Turkish Middle East, working long hard hours to do so. It was probably because of this that now, with Townshend already locked in Kut, he was given a new assignment. To the relief of his Cairo colleagues, he was sent to the Mesopotamian front to work on maps there, especially those assembled by means of the new craft of aerial photography. But soon after being installed in his new headquarters, a moored steamer on the Tigris, he met Aubrey Herbert, now a captain; a week later the two men, accompanied by Colonel Beach, Townshend's Intelligence Officer, were on their way to meet the Turkish commander, Khalil Pasha, in order to try to negotiate the payment of that extraordinary tribute.

A wait in no-man's-land, the sun a harder hammer than artillery, a blindfolded march, a blindfolded ride (though Lawrence refused that and walked) and finally the commander's tent and Khalil Pasha – 'a square chin and mouth like a trap', Herbert wrote of him. French was still the language of civilized diplomacy and Lawrence spoke it fluently – far better than he ever spoke Arabic. For hours the hopeless discussion continued, while in Kut Townshend in a spatter of explosions destroyed as much of his equipment as he could. Before that strange bargaining in Khalil's tent could drag into another day, the British and Indian forces in Kut had surrendered; twelve thousand prisoners were taken – seven in every ten of them would die in captivity. The only gain for the British was Lawrence's secret report on Khalil, assessing his character, his staff, his moods and his views.

Then the summer heat struck, the Mesopotamian war slowed and halted. In May, Lawrence was back again in Cairo. A month later Hussein, the Sherif of Mecca, perhaps improvidently and without sufficient outside backing, suddenly flung his sons and tattered armies openly against the Turks. The British had promised some help, but it had not yet arrived. The Sherifian forces, doing without it, overran the Turkish garrison in Mecca itself; they took Jiddah, they took Yenbo and Rabegh; at Medina, their energy finally ran out, their enterprise received a set-back from which it might never have recovered. Success had rallied some who had doubted; Turkish obduracy at Medina, the strength of their numbers and of their fortifications, turned some who had seemed steadfast into doubters.

Among the doubters from the beginning had been General Murray, Maxwell's successor as commander in the Middle East, and Hussein's rebuff at Medina almost confirmed him in his suspicion that the subsidies Britain had agreed to pay these volatile revolutionaries were nothing but a waste of money and supplies. Just as the British military caste had always had a respect for the professionalism of the Germans, so those with Middle Eastern experience were full of praise for their enemy, the Turks. The group of whom Lawrence was a junior member, however – Storrs and George Lloyd and the rest – thought very differently.

Storrs, indeed, was the man who had been given the task of turning down Hussein's pre-war request for help against Turkey, which had been brought to Cairo during a visit by his son and representative, Abdullah. Since the outbreak of the war, he had, with Kitchener's support, reopened secret negotiations with the Sherifiate and even passed on a vague assurance of British support in the Hashemite cause if the 'Arab nation', as it was phrased, agreed to help Britain in its struggle. (This idea of an 'Arab nation' was of course to beguile Lawrence too, although in practice he, like the rest of the Cairo experts, thought exclusively in Hashemite and even in Sherifian terms; the pro-Turkish Yemenis, the puritan and powerful Wahabi sect under Ibn Saud and various other tribes and groupings were either paid to keep still or simply disregarded.) Then, in mid-1915, Hussein had demanded as a

A typical Arab patrol
on the march.

71

Sir Henry McMahon, the British High Commissioner in Egypt: the portrait is by William Roberts. McMahon, a man of integrity, was put into a difficult position in his dealings with Hussein by the lack of communications between London, Cairo and New Delhi, where the Government of India supported Hussein's rival, Ibn Saud.

OPPOSITE The 'crooked house' at Jiddah, photographed from the balcony of the British Legation. It was here that the British and French Legations fought their diplomatic battle for control of the Arab revolt.

reward for his proposed venture against the Turks an enormous slice of territory, almost all the Arab-speaking lands between the borders of Persia, the shores of the Mediterranean and the Persian Gulf. Sir Henry McMahon, the British High Commissioner in Egypt, prepared after the collapse of the Dardanelles offensive to offer anyone anything, had accepted almost all this demand, although large parts of Syria were to be exempted and French interests were to be considered in any final settlement.

While Kitchener (who died on the day of Hussein's first rising) and McMahon had thus given the Sherif at least semi-official assurances of great future reward, the secret Sykes-Picot agreement between France and Britain had been signed in May 1916. This proceeded on a more traditional and imperialist basis, carving up the whole area into zones and apportioning these in ways that

74

seemed good to Paris and London (and St Petersburg and even, later, Rome). There was the 'Blue' zone, north of Acre and west of Damascus, which would be run by France, and a 'Red' zone stretching from the Persian Gulf along the river valleys to beyond Baghdad, which would be British; there was Zone 'A', a triangle based on Aleppo and including that town, Homs, Damascus and stretching to Lake Tiberias, which would be under French influence, though nominally independent, and there was Zone 'B', east of the Dead Sea and the Jordan Valley, which would be nominally independent but under British influence. Palestine would come under a British, French and Russian condominium, Russia by herself would take the Dardanelles, including Constantinople, and the area around Erzerum and Trebizond, while Italy, a late-comer to this premature dismemberment of the Ottoman enemy, was offered Smyrna and southern Anatolia, as well as a hastily demarcated zone of influence naturally marked 'C'.

There were thus contradictions in the Allied approach to Hussein right from the beginning, although there seems little doubt that as far as London was concerned the Sykes-Picot agreement came closer to their intentions than any *ad hoc* handing out of crowns and territories to temporary allies. These contradictions were compounded by the fact that the Indian Government in Delhi, viceregal, traditionalist and naturally obsessed with its routes to the west, was stubbornly against anything so unpredictable as an independent Arab state right across these lines of communication. Both the naval forces employed and one of the Mesopotamian armies were directly under its control. The High Commission in Cairo was, of course, under the Foreign Office, while the successive commanders based on Cairo, Maxwell, Murray and Allenby, were directed by the War Office. Such actual troops as were finally put down in the Hejaz (the area between Mecca and Medina east of the Red Sea) were directed from Khartoum and came under the control of the governor of the Sudan. The War Office co-ordinated this effort with the greater one of the Egyptian Expeditionary Force, and of course the War Cabinet, from the end of 1916 under Lloyd George, had the final overseeing responsibility. It is from this welter of conflicting commands and promises, ambitions and priorities, that Lawrence would finally emerge bitterly proclaiming the betrayal of the Arabs.

In these preliminaries to the Arab uprising, however, Lawrence had played only a small part. He had certainly written to Hogarth in March 1915, about all 'the little powers' which Delhi's diplomacy

OPPOSITE Sir Mark Sykes: in January 1916 he negotiated with the Frenchman Georges Picot the Sykes–Picot agreement. Lawrence saw him as 'a bundle of prejudices, intuitions, half-sciences', capable of both advancing and retarding the Arab cause.

75

A portrait of Storrs by Eric Kennington. Lawrence wrote of him: 'His shadow would have covered our work and British policy in the East like a cloak, had he been able to deny himself the world, and to prepare his mind and body with the sternness of an athlete for a great fight.'

had up till then kept suspended in a precarious balance of power, 'I want to pull them all together, & to roll up to Syria by way of the Hedjaz in the name of the Sherif'; but that 'I want' was little more than play-acting in so junior an officer. He was then in any case pinning his hopes on Ibn Ali el Idrissi, the ruler of Asir, who, although in the pay of the British, proved less than the heroic leader Lawrence thought him. And he had as his main intention not the defeat of Turkey but a rush to Damascus in order to 'biff the French out of all hope of Syria'. Now, however, he became one of the most eloquent champions of Hussein's revolt, his enthusiasm not only manifest but frequently and intemperately

76

voiced – he was not a man to restrain himself just because protocol demanded it. And in the first months of 1916 he wrote a memorandum which foreshadows the war he was to fight. He headed it *The Conquest of Syria: if Complete*, and in it pointed out that Hussein was

. . . held down by Turkish money – which we, via Egypt or India, could replace with interest – and by a Turkish Army Corps. The only way of ridding ourselves of this is by cutting the Hejaz line. . . . The Bedouin tribes hate the railway which has reduced their annual tolls and way-leaves; and would help us cut it. This cutting can be done by occupying Deraa if Damascus is neutralized: at Amman, if Jerusalem can be passed, by blowing up a viaduct: and at Maan by an occupation.

It was not in the event to be as simple as he had made it sound.

It had been not Lawrence but Storrs, Hogarth and another Arab Bureau officer, Colonel Cornwallis, who had in May 1916 made the journey into the Hejaz to meet and negotiate with Abdullah. It was only now that the chance appeared for Lawrence to take an active part, and that chance an unofficial one. His friend Storrs was setting off again to visit Abdullah, and Lawrence asked for ten days' leave in order to go with him. By now he had irritated so many of the senior officers at the Cairo headquarters that they were only too pleased to let him go. On 13 October 1916 Storrs, Lawrence and their little delegation embarked on the auxiliary cruiser *Lama*, on their way to Jiddah, Abdullah and legend.

Abdullah, painted by
Eric Kennington. Lawrence
felt that Abdullah's
character, indolent,
calculating and ambitious
by turns, did not fit him
for the role of prophet
of the Arab cause.

Ali, painted by Eric
Kennington. Lawrence
warmed to this brother,
so different in temperament
from Abdullah. Well read
and honest where Abdullah
was devious, he was
however handicapped
by consumption.

3 The Grand Illusion

The Hejaz show is a quaint one, the like of which
has hardly been on earth before, and no one not
of it can appreciate how difficult it is to run.
However, it has gone forward, and history will
call it a success. . . . All my memories of it are
pleasant . . . and if ever I can get my book on it
out, I'll try to make other people see it.

To Colonel C. E. Wilson, from Akaba, 2 September 1917

THE REVOLT OF THE SHERIF had run out of momentum; there were defections from his forces, rumours of Turkish preparations for a counter-attack out of Medina. Lawrence had been told that Abdullah was the guiding intelligence of Hussein's struggle, but when he met him, he was not over-impressed. Abdullah seemed too urbane, too welcoming, too chubby – 'I began to suspect him of a constant cheerfulness,' as he put it in *Seven Pillars of Wisdom*. Abdullah, according to Storrs, was rather more impressed with Lawrence. Talk had turned to the location of different units of the Turkish army; Lawrence, who had spent over a year interrogating prisoners and preparing maps, 'at once stated exactly which unit was in each position, until Abdullah turned to me in amazement: "Is this man God, to know everything?"' If there was irony behind the question, no one has recorded it.

PREVIOUS PAGES An Arab patrol, flying the Sherifian flag, marching across the desert, possibly led by Lawrence.

It was as a result of this admiration, in fact, that Abdullah was persuaded to write a letter of introduction for Lawrence to carry to the Emir Feisal. Abdullah had wanted British troops to land and keep safe the port of Rabegh; Lawrence agreed to represent these views to the authorities in Cairo, but was very doubtful whether any such reinforcements could or should be landed. He wanted, he said, to see the situation in Rabegh for himself and then from there to travel on to a meeting with Feisal. Abdullah agreed, but, contacted by telephone, Sherif Hussein proved more suspicious: what were the British after, sending representatives here and there across his domains? It was Storrs, the professionally charming diplomat, the hardened negotiator, who finally persuaded Hussein to give his permission.

At Rabegh, Hussein's eldest son, Ali, received with small enthusiasm his father's instructions to have Lawrence guided to

The British Residency at Cairo.

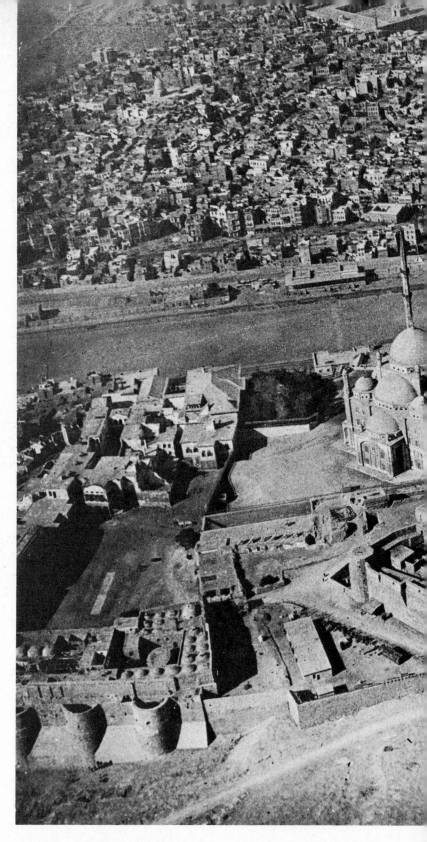

An aerial view of Cairo taken
in about 1925.

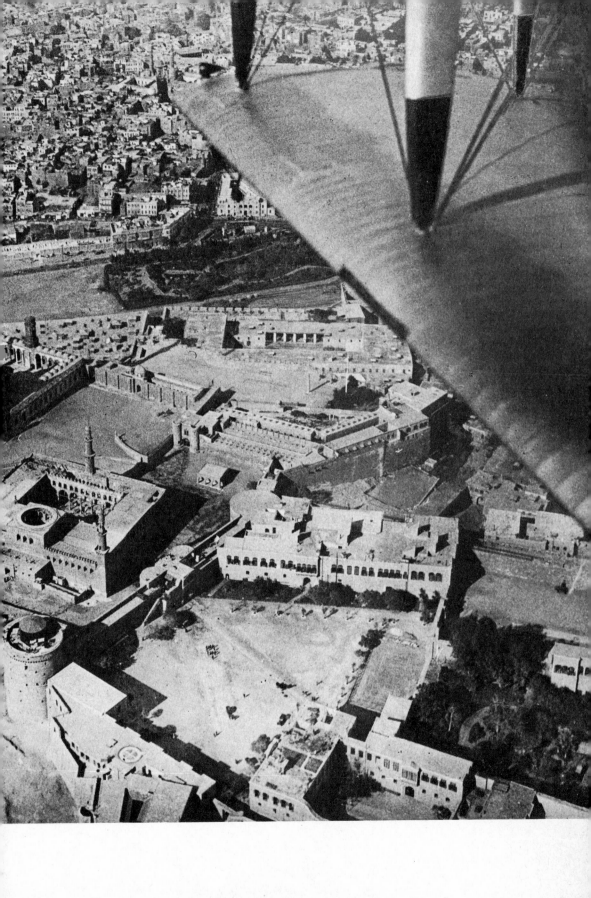

Feisal's camp, but could not disobey parental authority. He gave
him a guide and bodyguard named Tafas to see him safely through
the nearby territories of tribes now friendly to the Turks, and it
was in his charge that, two days and nights later, Lawrence reached
Wadi Safra, where, at Hamra, Feisal was awaiting him. 'Tafas said
something to a slave who stood there with silver-hilted sword in
hand,' Lawrence wrote in *Seven Pillars of Wisdom*. 'He led me to
an inner court, on whose further side, framed between the uprights
of a black doorway, stood a white figure waiting tensely for me.

Feisal with his Ageyli
bodyguard. According to
Lawrence, the men of this
tribe had white hands and
were 'too beautiful' to be
used as labourers.

I felt at first glance that this was the man I had come to Arabia
to seek. . . .' Later, Lawrence describes Feisal – a man of thirty-one
who looked older, with 'dark, appealing eyes' and 'hollow cheeks
deeply lined and puckered with reflection'; he was 'tall, graceful
and vigorous, with the most beautiful gait, and a royal dignity of
head and shoulders'.

So these two men met, in the first moment of their long,
bitter-sweet, love-hate connection, the tall gaunt Emir and the
yellow-haired, gentian-eyed, amateur soldier, short, sinewy,

87

narrow-shouldered, his oddity of appearance as misleading as was, in some ways, Feisal's manifest nobility, coming together now to begin their short years of violence, their doomed union, and all the hope and bloodshed, the anger, ambition, broken trust and sheer black tragedy that these would produce. Feisal showed him into a room. Both men sat. In the shadows, other men waited, cross-legged, watchful. Feisal murmured some politeness about the journey, then fell silent. Lawrence regarded him, waiting.

'And do you like our place here in Wadi Safra?' Feisal asked at last.

Lawrence plunged. 'Well; but it is far from Damascus.'

Such hastiness silenced the room. Then Feisal smiled. 'Praise be to God, there are Turks nearer us than that.'

After that, the talk between them was easier, both that day and during the rest of his visit. Feisal and his lieutenants spoke of the failure before Medina, where they had been swept aside for all

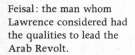

Feisal: the man whom Lawrence considered had the qualities to lead the Arab Revolt.

their impetuosity and courage by the superior armaments and implacable discipline of Fakhri Pasha's Turkish garrison. Artillery had broken them, body and spirit, and Fakhri's massacre of nearby villagers had given an edge of horror to their self-disgust. An Egyptian artillery unit had been sent from the Sudan to support Feisal's army, but their German guns were old and had not the range to make a satisfactory reply to the kind of questions Turkish gunners were asking. Other British supplies had been stolen by the defected tribes around Rabegh, and the British as a result had stopped sending more. Yet with new guns and more ammunition, Feisal said, he and his brothers would make another attack on Medina, either to take it or at the least to disrupt any Turkish preparations for a counter-attack against the Sherif.

After a short tour of the bare, surrounding countryside – 'the dawn showed gentle valleys of sand with strange hills of lava hemming us about' – Lawrence rode on camel-back down through the long sand ridges, the banks of shingle and the shade of palm-grove and acacia to where the bulk of Jebel Rudhwa marked the position of the sea-port, Yenbo. There he boarded the *Suva*, and so travelled with his tidings to Jiddah under the disapproving eye of Captain Boyle, one of the many who felt that there was something almost immoral in a white man's taking to Arab head-gear and robes. The local naval commander, Admiral Wemyss, with whom Lawrence travelled on to Khartoum to make his report to Sir Reginald Wingate, governor of the Sudan, was another such,

The Government palace and garden at Khartoum: this palace was built on the spot where General Gordon died. The photograph was taken in 1933.

OVERLEAF A view over Wadi Ruum, showing Bedouin tents.

89

although a strong supporter of the Arab uprising; he thought
Lawrence's easy acceptance of Arab dress a kind of affectation and
the clothes themselves 'fancy dress'. For Lawrence, however, this
was another of his exercises in conspicuous anonymity, allowing
him to feel at one with aliens from whom he differed so funda-
mentally in appearance, and to feel alien among colleagues from
whom he felt so different in temperament, while claiming all the
while that his reasons for wearing the dress were severely practical.

Wingate, aware of the inactivity in the Hejaz and worried by it,
was pleased to learn that Feisal intended a new attack on Medina.
What was needed, he thought, was an Anglo-French force to
stiffen the Sherif's armies and to form with them a combined force
with which to drive northwards into Syria. Lawrence disagreed,
and vehemently – the more so as this army would have been led
by Colonel Brémond, a French soldier of some reputation, upholder
of French interests in the Middle East and in that role a delicate
intriguer as well as a hard negotiator, a man who was known to
be Abdullah's friend, and one to whom Lawrence took a mulish
dislike. Ostensibly this was because of his suspicions of French
intentions in the Middle East, but one may suspect that there was
more than a little personal jealousy in his antipathy to the French
officer.

The Hejaz, he had determined, should be his own arena. He
had found his king and he would crown him. Feisal was to be the
man under whom the Arabs should rally, and Lawrence would be
the one to build his platform, set up his throne. Of course, he may
not yet have had these ambitions clearly in his mind; he was for
the moment intoxicated by his new power as the man – to quote
Wingate's cable to Cairo – 'of great experience and knowledge
who has just returned from visit to Feisal's camp. . . .' But he
fought with all his energy against Brémond's proposals, and half
brought Wingate round to his point of view. The first essential
was to supply Feisal with guns and ammunition so that the Arabs
themselves might continue their war against the Turks – and for
their own liberty.

In Cairo, Murray, the c-in-c, had a much less affectionate or
respectful view of the Arabs than either Admiral Wemyss – who
had already done a great deal to help Hussein's struggle – or
Wingate. It seemed likely that he would disagree with Britain's
sending any really effective aid to the Arabs. In the event, he was
more amenable than Lawrence had expected. Lawrence had sent
a report to General Clayton, who was head of Military Intelligence

in Cairo, setting out his views with his usual turbulent dogmatism. The Arab tribes, he pointed out, would with new supplies be able to engage the Turks for months, but if a force of foreigners landed, even if they were supposed to be allies, they would disperse into their complex wilderness and leave the newcomers isolated. These counter-proposals to the plans of Brémond and Wingate seemed immediately attractive to Cairo because the hard-pressed British had no real desire to commit units of an over-extended army to an adventure in the Hejaz.

But at this stage Lawrence seems to have had no intention of taking to camel-back at the side of his new idol, Emir Feisal. He was an Intelligence Officer, one who could assess, synthesize, manipulate; he was not a warrior, a man to be buried in mere action. It was probably something of a shock to him therefore when General Clayton a few days later gave him the task of acting as Feisal's military adviser; he argued that he hated responsibility, had no experience of handling men – 'They were not my medium: I was not practised in that technique' – hated soldiering and was not in any case a regular officer of the kind Wingate had already asked for to undertake that task. There was no time to wait for anyone else, Clayton replied, there had to be connection between Feisal and Cairo, and Lawrence was the man Feisal had already met. He would serve under the senior British officer with the Sherifiate, Colonel Joyce. Argument ceased; Lawrence had to go. Was he really as reluctant as *Seven Pillars of Wisdom* suggests? He was neither a coward nor afraid of hardship; on the other hand, he enjoyed the urbane pleasures open to a cultivated young man in even a war-time capital. He had books to read, intelligent companions to converse with, the unpredictable excitements of his work. He was editor of the *Arab Bulletin*, a secret and thus highly influential periodical, founded in June 1916, perhaps at Lawrence's own suggestion, published by the Arab Bureau and circulated for the information of an exclusive handful of officials. It would have been neither unlikely nor discreditable if he had wavered at the prospect of what must have seemed a kind of exile.

Towards the end of November, however, Lawrence landed at Yenbo. He must at that moment have felt fairly confident. He knew that along the coast at Rabegh the British had now based four warplanes as well as a mixed bag of some twenty pieces of artillery, that with them there were nine hundred men of the Camel Corps and three hundred other troops seconded from the Egyptian army, while Aziz al-Masri, an Egyptian whom Hussein

Yenbo: Lawrence's house is on the right in this photograph.

had made his Minister of War, was trying to organize the two thousand men of his regular army. Other Arab levies were drilling at Yenbo itself, where Captain Garland, an officer seconded to the Hejaz despite persistent heart trouble, was enthusiastically educating the Sherifians in the destructive uses of dynamite. It was he who taught Lawrence, too, his later familiarity with high explosives. And it is Garland whom Lawrence credits with the earliest raids on the Hejaz Railway, thus becoming the man who 'had derailed the first train and broken the first culvert in Arabia'.

It was in good spirits therefore that Lawrence set out from Yenbo to reach Feisal at his headquarters, so that the descent from this mood was all the more abrupt and bitter when that night he suddenly found a world that should have been deserted filled with a confusion of men, camels, tents and fires. The Turks had moved before the Sherifians; they had struck towards the coast and so prevented the armies of Hussein's sons from coming together in preparation for their own assault. Feisal had been almost trapped in Wadi Safra, Zeid had barely escaped capture, and both Ali advancing from Rabegh and Abdullah from Mecca had been checked before properly on the move. Now Feisal was in Wadi Yenbo, holding the approaches to that suddenly threatened port. As a result, the brothers were bickering, their men were deserting and, what was worse, taking their weapons with them. The only centre of hope was Feisal himself, steady in the face of near disaster and a steadier of others. He, with Lawrence beside him, now set himself to reviving the morale of those he led. Slowly, the bubbling of panic subsided; the British instructors who had already arrived intensified their training. Defences were prepared against the Turkish column, now expected almost any day.

It was eleven o'clock one night when patrols saw the Turks some three miles from the town and gave the alarm. Garland called out the garrison, using a crier to summon them, and without any of their usual yells or encouraging shots they went to their places. All was silence and starlight and shadow. Then, from the warships in the harbour, the blue-white beams of searchlights stretched suddenly across the darkness, picking out the bare approaches, the bleak, uncovered slopes. Unnerved, the attackers waited, wavered, turned away – 'and that night, I believe, the Turks lost their war', Lawrence comments.

When Lawrence arrived in Rabegh, to discuss with Colonel Wilson, Wingate's representative in the Hejaz, what should be done to consolidate this success, he found Brémond there instead;

Feisal and his army coming
in to Yenbo in December
1916. Here the Turks lost
their nerve in the stillness
of night and retreated.

Colonel Wilson's staff. Wilson was the representative in the Hejaz of Sir Reginald Wingate, governor of the Sudan. He was sent to Jiddah as military adviser and head of the British mission to Sherif Hussein, but this was not publicly broadcast.

soon the bearded Frenchman was once more trying to persuade Lawrence to his own policy of an Anglo-French expedition. The Arab revolution, he said, had come and gone, and the Sherifians could no longer be depended on. In any case, if Hussein had to rely upon an Allied detachment, it would weaken his political position; he would after the war be unable to claim more than Medina and the Hejaz as his reward. Lawrence, however, was now committed to seeing Feisal in Damascus, such a triumph being the only way in which, under Sykes-Picot, the Arabs would be able to set up their independent kingdoms. Already, if *Seven Pillars of Wisdom* is to be believed, he saw himself not only as a British officer seeking 'to biff the French out of Syria', while doing the same to the Turks, but also as a voice and mind at the service of Arab – or at least Hashemite – independence. Yet he knew all about the Sykes-Picot agreement, with its over- and undertones of imperialist ambition, its lordly handing out of zones and drawing up of frontiers; more, he himself had advocated as early as January 1916, in a secret paper, *The Politics of Mecca*, that the Sherifiate states, once set up, should 'remain in a state of political mosaic, a tissue of small jealous principalities incapable of cohesion', in order to render them harmless to Britain. Even at this stage therefore, had he allowed himself to give the matter any thought, he must have realized that in the unpredictable earthquake which had hit the Middle East, he was straddling a widening abyss. But increasingly one gets the impression that his present involvement had swept aside his previous coolly analytic attitude.

Wilson, arriving from Jiddah, brought the news that Murray was after all considering precisely the kind of force Brémond

Colonel Wilson, drawn by Eric Kennington.

wanted, that a brigade was being held in Egypt for the purpose and that Lawrence's friend and colleague, Colonel Newcombe, would soon be on his way to work out how such a body might best co-operate with the Arab armies. If there was to be independent Sherifiate movement, it would have to be soon. It was decided to send Abdullah to threaten the Hejaz Railway, that long strip of vulnerable steel between Damascus and Medina upon which the latter's Turkish garrison relied for their supplies. Feisal, meanwhile, with naval support, would capture Wejh, the last port on that stretch of the Red Sea Coast still in Turkish hands. If it fell, Akaba, five hundred miles farther north, would be the only harbour through which Turks could land supplies. Full of enthusiasm, the two British officers put this plan to Feisal, but the Emir was lukewarm. He was, after all, safe where he was. It was a promise of British naval support for the defence of his bases which finally persuaded him.

On 14 January 1917, Feisal's army set out for Wejh; meanwhile, a British squadron under Captain Boyle prepared its own seaborne attack. It was a fortnight exactly to the planned assault, when Feisal's ten thousand tribesmen and Boyle's Arab regulars and British marines were due to converge upon the unhappy port. 'The march became rather splendid and barbaric,' Lawrence wrote. 'First rode Feisal in white . . . myself on his left in white and scarlet, behind us three banners of faded crimson silk. . . .' Its splendour lasted a week, during which their column covered a hundred miles. Then, surrounded by strangers, short of food and inhibited by unfamiliar terrain, they began to lag behind schedule. When there was only a day left before the planned attack, Newcombe, who had been happy to travel with them, agreed to ride on ahead. There was a *rendezvous* due with the *Hardinge*, one of Boyle's ships, charged with the task of provisioning Feisal's column; perhaps moving on his own he would be able to reach the agreed spot, Habban, in time, and persuade Boyle to delay his attack until Feisal's force was in position.

The next day was cold, a sharp wind blew into their faces, they had to scramble across an endless network of dry *wadis*. And all day their despondency grew as the sound of heavy firing drummed across the sky from where Wejh lay ahead of them. They found the *Hardinge* waiting for them, and Lawrence heard on board that Boyle, afraid the Turks would bring in reinforcements, had ploddingly decided to attack as though Feisal's army were actually there. Three days later, the Sherifiate force finally reached Wejh,

Feisal's army approaching Wejh in January 1917. Lawrence and the Sherifiate
force arrived to find that Vickery had already led the Arab regulars in defeating the Turks.

OPPOSITE A portrait of Lawrence in Arab dress, by James McBey.

ABOVE General Allenby: a portrait by James McBey. Lawrence wrote of Allenby's understanding and commented that he could satisfy even 'his very greediest servant'.

ABOVE A view of the wells at Wejh.
OPPOSITE Colonel Newcombe (right) with one of the local Arab sheikhs at Wejh in January 1917.

104

to find that town attacked, overrun and ransacked. Lawrence's bitterness was made complete when he discovered that Major Vickery, one of Newcombe's staff officers, a professional soldier who not only despised such amateur stopgap officers as himself but also spoke Arabic with a fluency he was never to match, and whom he considered as a result a rival as dangerous as Brémond, had been in charge of the Arab regulars during their successful action. Some twenty men had been killed in the assault and Vickery 'was satisfied, but I could not share his satisfaction'.

Lawrence felt that even if the two-hundred-strong Turkish garrison had escaped, 'it would not have mattered the value of an Arab life.' It was, after all, as a base that the port was wanted – 'the smashing and killing in it had been wanton.'

The overall position, however, was now more settled – and settled in the Sherifiate favour. The strength of the revolt was clearly apparent. The coastline as far as Wejh, some two hundred miles north of Medina, lay under the control of Feisal. The Hejaz Railway, a hundred miles or so inland, stretched vulnerable to attack. The necessity to bring in the Allied force waiting in Egypt had been staved off – and indeed Brémond, still in Jiddah, received the news of Feisal's success with indignation. He understood its significance; worse, he had not been informed that the attack was planned; worst of all, he received a restrained reprimand from Joffre, in Paris, who felt that both British and Arabs were beginning to suspect that Brémond, because of his own plans for the French in Syria, was trying to keep the Hussein uprising penned in the Hejaz. If these suspicions became entrenched, the French Commander-in-Chief felt, it might have 'serious consequences on the development of our plans in the Levant', a guarded phrase which leads one to think that Lawrence's doubts about his allies were not entirely unfounded.

Since it was indeed Brémond's intention to restrict Sherifiate activities to the Hejaz, and since he was a large, bearded, forceful man strong in his convictions, he allowed himself to be restrained neither by Feisal's new standing nor by France's present alarm. This he attributed, in any case, to reports coming in the first place from Lawrence himself, and he knew very well how things stood between himself and this diminutive British officer in Feisal's train. He travelled to Cairo, intent on arguing his case once more, his plan this time to land the Anglo-French force he had proposed in Akaba. As he pointed out to Lawrence himself when they met in the Egyptian capital, it was not only the Turks' last port on the Red Sea coast, it was also the nearest to that Hejaz Railway which kept the Medina garrison supplied, and it lay usefully behind the left flank of the Allied army then based on Beersheba.

Lawrence was not only suspicious of his intentions, he was also dubious about the scheme's practicality; behind Akaba lay a glowering escarpment, hills from which any invasion could be overlooked and any landing force dominated. It was not from the sea, he thought, that Akaba could be taken. His primary objection, however, was the reverse of those ideas which prompted Brémond's proposal – he knew as well as the Frenchman that, if the Sherifiate forces were ever to achieve that hoped-for, climactic entry into Damascus, their path lay through Akaba. If another force took the port, Feisal's route to the north would be blocked and his task pre-empted. Despite his new and agreeable standing in Cairo, therefore, as an important partner in an unexpectedly successful enterprise, Lawrence left the capital to return to Wejh and Feisal. The Emir, unaware of Brémond's double-edged intentions, had to be persuaded to resist the Frenchman's proposals, plausible but dangerous to his cause – 'I had not warned Feisal that Brémond was a politician,' as he wrote later.

It is clear from all this complexity of plot, plan and conference that for Lawrence, as for Brémond, the war against Turkey was little more than a necessary chore which lay between them and the real task. Brémond's intentions were clear – he wanted a wide French interest in the Middle East, and particularly in Syria, with for himself perhaps a governorship, a high reputation, a paragraph in the history books and a distinguished retirement. In these ambitions he was opposed by the wary Arabists and imperially minded diplomats who staffed the relevant British offices in Cairo. But Lawrence's opposition was never theirs; he was not unaware of Feisal's connection with the British, nor that with the Hashemites in power British interests would probably be protected, but it was not this that seems now to have animated him. He had a vision of a great Arab-speaking state, its capital Damascus, with Feisal as its king. It should of course be friendly to Britain, at best even a member of the Commonwealth. But he had sunk himself in that dream of Arab unity which still haunts and still eludes the presidents and prime ministers of the eastern Mediterranean. In them the dream is natural – they are Arabs. What set it whirling in Lawrence's mind?

The theme of Lawrence's life had been apartness. He had always been different, even from his brothers. He had always been solitary. After the war apartness would go further and turn into escape; he wanted to obliterate, to an extent at least, the person that he was, or had been. In Mesopotamia before the war he had found a new freedom, and he had found love. (Again one thinks of Byron, burning to liberate – and also from the Turks – his beloved Greeks, among whom he himself had always felt so free.) With Dahoum, or on his own, walking through the bleak, sun-battered landscapes of his choice, he had become someone different from that T. E. Lawrence who had had in Oxford to assert himself

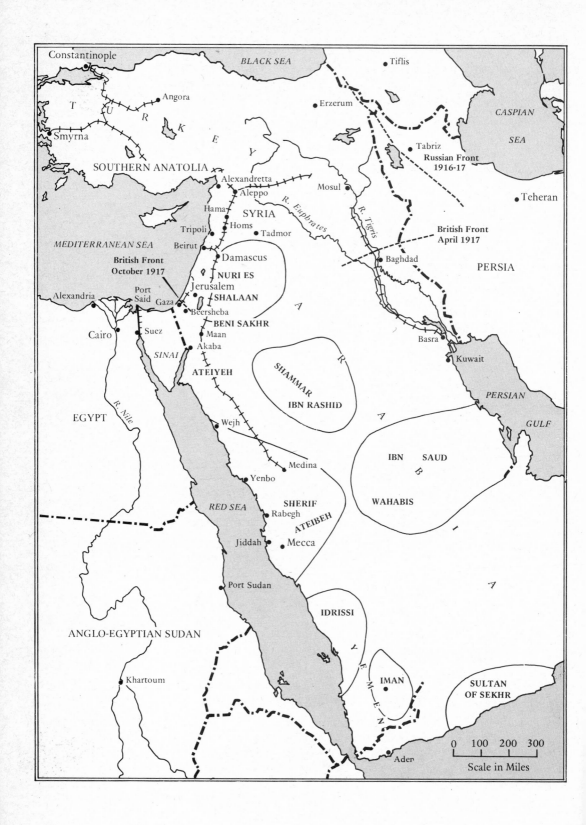

Constantinople ·   *BLACK SEA*   · Tiflis

· Angora

T   U   R   K   E   Y

Smyrna ·   · Erzerum   *CASPIAN*

SEA

SOUTHERN ANATOLIA   · Tabriz

Russian Front
1916-17

· Alexandretta   · Mosul   · Teheran

· Aleppo   *R. Euphrates*

Hama ·   SYRIA   *R. Tigris*

Tripoli ·   · Homs

British Front
April 1917

MEDITERRANEAN SEA   Beirut ·   · Tadmor

· Damascus   PERSIA

British Front   **NURI ES**   · Baghdad

October 1917   Jerusalem   **SHALAAN**

Alexandria ·   Port   Gaza ·   · Beersheba

Said ·   **BENI SAKHR**   A

Cairo ·   · Suez   · Maan   Basra ·

SINAI   · Akaba   · Kuwait

ATEIYEH   R

EGYPT   *R. Nile*   SHAMMAR   *PERSIAN*

IBN RASHID   A   *GULF*

· Wejh

IBN   SAUD

· Medina   B

· Yenbo

RED SEA   **SHERIF**   WAHABIS

· Rabegh   **ATEIBEH**   I

Jiddah ·   · Mecca

ANGLO-EGYPTIAN SUDAN   · Port Sudan   A

IDRISSI

Y
E
· Khartoum   M   **IMAN**   **SULTAN**
E   **OF SEKHR**
N

· Aden   0   100   200   300

Scale in Miles

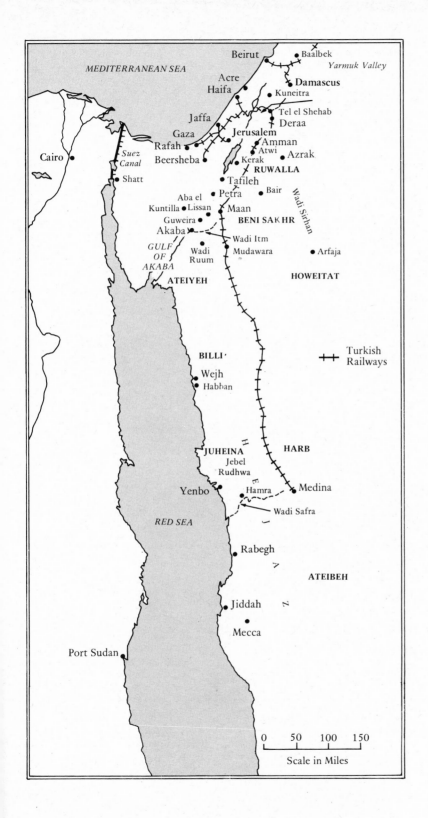

MEDITERRANEAN SEA

Beirut
Baalbek
Yarmuk Valley

Acre
Haifa
Damascus
Kuneitra

Jaffa
Tel el Shehab
Deraa

Gaza
Jerusalem
Amman
Rafah
Atwi
Azrak

Cairo
Beersheba
Kerak
RUWALLA

Suez
Canal

Shatt
Tafileh

Aba el
Petra
Bair

Kuntilla • Lissan
Maan

Guweira
BENI SAKHR

Akaba
Wadi Itm

GULF
OF
AKABA
Wadi
Ruum
Mudawara
Arfaja

ATEIYEH
HOWEITAT

BILLI
Turkish
Railways
Wejh
Habban

JUHEINA
HARB
Jebel
Rudhwa

Yenbo
Hamra
Medina

RED SEA
Wadi Safra

Rabegh

ATEIBEH

Jiddah

Mecca

Port Sudan

0   50   100   150

Scale in Miles

through endless unimportant eccentricities. He had escaped – but only for a while. Now, with Feisal, he might make that escape permanent. He would help him to a throne, he would become part of the Arabs' central enterprise, they would accept him as one of themselves.

Of course, that effort failed and he learned soon enough that it would have to. His public attitude to his attempt at becoming an Arab among Arabs is contained in a 1917 manual demonstrating how political officers should bear themselves in these alien tents; all seems to be calculation and considered acting. But there are echoes of his inner hopes to be found in the melancholy with which he regarded their disappointment: 'If I could not assume their character, I could at least conceal my own . . .', he was to write in *Seven Pillars of Wisdom*. And again, 'A man who gives himself to be a possession of aliens . . . may imitate them so well that they spuriously imitate him back again. Then he is giving away his own environment: pretending to theirs; and pretences are hollow, worthless things.' And once more, 'In my case, the efforts for these years to live in the dress of Arabs, and to imitate their mental foundations, quitted me of my English self. . . . At the same time, I could not sincerely take on the Arab skin: it was an affectation only.' These were insights he came to in time, but then, at Feisal's side, intoxicated by great ambitions, by his acceptance in these alien tents, by the power his position gave him, he is unlikely to have been fully aware of the contradictions in his role – or if he was, he must in his enthusiasm have thought that he could reconcile them.

It was therefore Feisal's interests that he was putting first when he hurried back to Wejh. It is not indeed certain whether the meeting he describes between Brémond and Feisal, with himself in gleeful attendance, ever occurred, or occurred when and in the way he wrote of it, but *Seven Pillars of Wisdom* is his own book, and nudges him perhaps inevitably nearer to the centre of the stage, despite his own insistence that the story had no hero. So that Feisal's steadfastness, Brémond's insistence and eventual discomfiture, may be no more than a literary shaping of what ought to have happened; what is true is that it accurately and dramatically sets out the arguments and the fact that Brémond was the loser, and so helps to establish the logical basis for Feisal's next move. That would be, of course, the sweep upon Akaba, which, Lawrence insisted, 'would be best taken by Arab irregulars descending from the interior without naval help'.

In order to move again, Feisal's army had to regroup and re-equip, and the next two months were spent in Wejh, organizing the distribution of the guns, stores, ammunition and money which Cairo was now supplying with an enthusiastic liberality. At the same time, new recruits appeared to strengthen the force – sinewy tribesmen who rode in, gaunt and spectral, from the dusty recesses of that country, and men of reputation come to add their energy to the leadership. Such chiefs of tribes and clans brought their people with them, for Feisal had money and weapons and perhaps fame to distribute and they wanted their share.

Lawrence, however, was setting off on a different mission. Intercepted Turkish cables had informed Murray's headquarters staff that the Medina garrison was about to be withdrawn, and they had become alarmed at the thought of the reinforcements this would mean for the army facing them on the Beersheba front (another twenty-five thousand troops, Lawrence estimates; Murray seems to have thought it about half that number). Clayton urged Lawrence to see that Medina was attacked again, or that its garrison be destroyed should it venture on its hazardous retreat. Feisal immediately shifted units to threaten the Hejaz Railway, its lines already harassed by the explosive forays of Newcombe and, separately, the French. It was Abdullah's forces, however, which lay outside Medina. Lawrence, therefore, rode south-eastward to Abdullah's camp, 125 miles away, his route through the bleak mountains which lie between coast and desert there. He was feverish again, weak with dysentery and suffering from boils. On the journey, he says, a quarrel arose, there was a killing at the end of it, the possibility of a blood feud and a long trail of death into the future. He decided to execute the murderer himself – 'At least no revenge could lie against my followers; for I was a stranger and kinless.' He was weak and nervous and had to shoot three times; shot by shot he describes this bungled execution. When he reached Abdullah's camp in Abu Markha, he collapsed into the delirium of fever.

When Lawrence recovered, he must have thought at first that he might have saved himself the journey, for Abdullah had lost his zest for the war. Lawrence wanted him to help cut the Hejaz Railway; Abdullah wanted to discuss the royal families of Europe or the battles of the Western Front. But Sherif Shakir, his second-in-command, was keen for action, and it was with him therefore that Lawrence set off to try to destroy the station at Aba el Naam. With them travelled Captain Raho, a French officer whom

Lawrence describes as 'a very hard-working and honest fellow', but whose presence is an indication of how much more under French, and therefore Brémond's, influence Abdullah was than Feisal. Aba el Naam was, as it turned out, too heavily defended for the numbers they had been able to raise and it was decided to mine the rails to north and south of it. The station was shelled; soon after, a locomotive left for the south, hit Lawrence's mine and halted, but machine-gunners who should have been in place were not and so the Turks were able to repair it; around the station, however, trucks were burning, the black smoke stretching into the morning sky to signal at least a partial success for the Arab attack. And for Lawrence the journey had its own significance: it was the first time during the war that he had himself reached that ramshackle railway line with which three armies were so obsessed – 'I dismounted and fingered its thrilling rails. . . .'

There was another such expedition, abortive at first, then more successful, before Lawrence finally returned to Abdullah's camp. He was still not happy in its atmosphere, however, and it is clear that he and the future king of Transjordania held a low opinion of each other. While Lawrence was there, a letter arrived from Brémond, warning Abdullah that everywhere the British were putting themselves in control of the Arabs and that his own position would soon be eroded. Lawrence countered this elegantly by saying that 'I hoped he would suspect our honesty when he found us backbiting our allies in private letters.' It was with little regret, on the whole, that he set out again to rejoin Feisal.

At Wejh, everything was going extravagantly well. There had arrived armoured Rolls-Royces from Egypt, the warplanes which had been stationed at Rabegh, experts of various sorts seconded from other units. And, soon after Lawrence's return, there was the unexpected arrival of a legend. A whispered message in Feisal's ear, a sudden sense of alertness, of expectation, Feisal 'with shining eyes, trying to be calm', turning to Lawrence with the explanation, 'Auda is here,' and then the appearance of Auda abu Tayi himself, a man perhaps in his fifties, but 'still strong and straight. . . . His face was magnificent in its lines and hollows. . . . He had married twenty-eight times, had been wounded thirteen times. . . . He himself had slain seventy-five men . . . in battle: and never a man except in battle.' He was the archetype of all desert raiders, a pirate of the waste lands, a fighter of endless desperate actions, but a man steeped in the traditions of a long-established code of honour – in short, already an anachronism even in those

OPPOSITE Sherif Shakir, the cousin of Abdullah and his second-in-command. He recruited a force taken mostly from the Ateibeh tribe to take part in Lawrence's assault on the Hejaz railway.

113

British aircraft grounded by a dust storm at Gayadah in 1916. This photograph shows the climatic conditions with which the fighter pilots were faced.

early decades of oil and technology, yet because of his reputation as well as his experience and courage a man of the greatest value to Feisal's cause. And Lawrence, watching these two men embrace, felt that in Auda Feisal, the far-sighted idealist, had found his warrior complement. Not only that, Auda's tribe, the Howeitat, a clan hardened in a hundred battles – many of them against the long-detested Turks – would be a potent addition to Feisal's fighting force.

Akaba now loomed larger, for Auda too had conceived the idea of taking it. Indeed, George Antonius in *The Arab Awakening* says categorically that he was the first to suggest this to Feisal; but in London and Khartoum the attack had already been discussed, and

114

Lawrence in conversation
with Auda abu Tayi, Sheikh
of the Howeitat tribe.
A seasoned bandit, he had
conducted numerous raids
against neighbouring tribes
and, particularly, the Turks.
Lawrence was amused by
the spectacle of this old
chief grinding his only pair
of dentures to powder
because they had been given
to him by Jemal Pasha.

Brémond and Newcombe had as a result spoken of it to the Emir months before. It is not clear whether Lawrence ever claimed, though others did so for him, that he had originated the idea of capturing Akaba and indeed so obvious was the strategic need to do so that many people must have seen it. What he perhaps could claim was that his was the plan upon which the action was based, and that it was his and Auda's enthusiasm which led to that attack being given preference over the assault on Medina suggested by Cairo. (Antonius, in his book, however, gives Auda all the credit for this, too, and says that Lawrence 'asked to go' on the expedition only 'as an emissary to the Arab leaders in Damascus'. But Antonius, as the Arabs' advocate, had his own axes to grind. Truth, as so often, may well be found between these conflicting attitudes.) Lawrence realized that Feisal's forces were no match for a disciplined army settled into prepared fortifications and that any frontal charge upon the guns of Medina would end in bloody disaster. What the tribesmen had on their side was speed, a knowledge of the country and the ability to live in it – in other words, the basic necessary equipment of a guerrilla force. There was, he felt, no point in using them to do the work of an army corps, the kind of work which Brémond's desired brigade might have done better. They would have to struggle for their own successes in their own way.

What he now suggested, therefore, was that he should leave the bulk of Feisal's men to do Cairo's bidding and concentrate on the Hejaz Railway and the Medina garrison, while he and a few companions travelled the two hundred miles which separated Wejh from Wadi Sirhan and the Howeitat heartlands. Feisal agreed, Auda was enthusiastic and, on 9 May 1917 Feisal's cousin and second-in-command, Sherif Nasir of Mecca, Lawrence and Auda beside him, led out their little group, some forty men carrying rifles, flour for sustenance and gold for the persuasion of their potential allies. For in Wadi Sirhan Lawrence and Auda hoped to gather a force which would sweep into Akaba from the unprotected east, the vulnerable landward side, so not only damaging the Turks but also presenting the Allies with a political *fait accompli*. It is clear from the nature and purpose of this plan that Lawrence was now much less a British officer than he was a proponent of Feisal's cause and that he was quite prepared to disregard the Cairo establishment in order to push the Arab interest.

It was now, too, that he seems to have become most at one with his companions. He was not yet beset by doubts or revulsion; his

OPPOSITE Sherif Nasir, Feisal's cousin and second-in-command. In his late twenties, Nasir was an asset to the Arab movement, though war was alien to his nature.

116

dream of an Arab kingdom and himself a power in it was still burgeoning; and in the meantime he had the day-by-day satisfaction of a difficult journey among men whom he respected and who, he felt, respected him. It was during this expedition that he unintentionally founded the nucleus of that exotic bodyguard which would later become so important a part of his legend, but which, with its nickname of 'Lawrence's Tulips', would be a source of bawdy humour for many.

Daud was young, handsome, strong and manly; Farraj was delicate, slim, almost girlish, certainly beautiful. It was Daud who approached Lawrence – Farraj by chance or frolic had burned down their tent, he was about to be beaten for it, Lawrence's intercession might save him. All that Lawrence could manage, however, was to get Daud to share Farraj's punishment, a solution at which the lad's reported delight seems extravagant. The next day 'two bent figures, with pain in their eyes' came limping to Lawrence – Daud and Farraj, come to offer themselves as men in Lawrence's service. Lawrence wanted no servants or followers, he says, but Farraj pleaded, 'all the woman of him evident in his longing', and 'mainly because they looked so young and clean', he took them on. 'They were', he wrote, 'an instance of the eastern boy and boy affection which the segregation of women made inevitable. Such friendships often led to manly loves of a depth and force beyond our flesh-steeped conceit.' However, with sexuality the relationship became 'give and take, unspiritual . . . like marriage'.

The days of their journey passed, the landscape strange, crater pitted, basalt-black, the heat a weight and a piercing torment, the world almost empty of natural life. Men appeared from time to time – Hornby, Newcombe's acolyte, 'a fair-haired, shaggy-bearded Englishman in tattered uniform', as obsessed as his chief with hoisting the tracks of the Hejaz Railway on the dust-plumes of endless explosions; a patrol of hostile tribesmen, defended by caution, speed and a crackle of rifle fire. Ten days from Wejh, they crossed the railway themselves, blowing up great lengths of track (Auda, to whom dynamite was new, composing poetry 'on its powerful glory') and tearing down telegraph poles. Then they were on the move again, and eight days later, their bodies dried by the furnace winds of the Arabian summer, their faces caked with dust, they reached the low, tamarisk-covered hills of Arfaja.

Travel, hard work and diplomacy still awaited them. A patrol of Shammar, a tribe long hostile to the Howeitat, caused them alarm and a passing skirmish. Auda pushed the party on, therefore,

118

in order to reach the main body of his people, which after three further days they did, to be met by the obligatory feast of welcome. Then, in order to secure his base, Auda travelled to a meeting with Nuri Shaalan, Emir of the Ruwalla and the Howeitat's neighbour. Feisal had suggested that Nuri should now declare for Turkey, so making it unlikely that any Turkish troops, badly needed elsewhere, would probe into his territories. Such an action would also make the Ruwalla into *de facto* allies of the Howeitat and thus unlikely to descend upon their villages once Auda's men had departed westward to Akaba. Sheikh Nuri proved amenable, and the benevolence with which the Turks thought he regarded them provided a screen behind which Auda's excited preparations could go ahead.

The excitement, indeed, threatened to get out of hand. Gold and the possibility of success against the Turks brought the tribesmen out in their hundreds. Not only that, as the force gathered, it became increasingly ambitious and, directed by Nesib el Bekri, a Syrian exiled and under sentence of death for the help he had given Feisal, began to clamour for a direct strike at Damascus. Lawrence was aghast; he was not ready yet for such a thrust: 'I pointed him in vain to Feisal yet in Wejh: to the British yet the wrong side of Gaza: to the new Turkish army massing in Aleppo. . . . I showed how we in Damascus would be unsupported. . . . But Nesib was towering above geography, and beyond tactics. . . .' It was only by mobilizing ancient religious, tribal and even personal rivalries that Lawrence was able to keep these ambitions at bay.

But, if *Seven Pillars of Wisdom* is to be believed, it was now, with his own enterprise building, that doubts about what he was doing began to penetrate Lawrence's certainties. As he roundly says, 'The Arab Revolution was begun on false pretences' – that is, on the conflict between such promises as McMahon's and the Sykes-Picot agreement. Challenged by Nuri Shaalan, who had got wind of these varying pledges, Lawrence temporized by advising the Arabs 'to trust the latest in date of the contradictions'. (Later, Bolshevik publication of all pre-revolutionary Russia's secret treaties would spread the knowledge of these 'contradictions' widely through the Arab world, giving rise to considerable disillusionment.) And it was as a result of this, he says, and because of his self-disgust at so deceiving people who looked to him for honourable leadership, that he 'vowed to make the Arab Revolt the engine of its own success' – that is, to make sure it became so successful that moral obligation would finally force the Allies to meet the Arab claims. This sounds suspiciously like clarity after the event, a formula for evading responsibility. Lawrence knew a larger world than that of Arab and Bedouin, and must have realized that no local success of the kind open to Feisal's guerrilla forces – forces which he had recognized were essentially and necessarily guerrilla – would ever be able to sway the bland, hard-headed empire-builders of London and Paris. The fact is that what distorted his position was his temperamental need to identify with the Sherifiate cause; without that, doubtless like all the other British officers involved in the Hejaz, he could have excused his double-minded deception of the Arabs by demonstrating his single-minded devotion to the Allies. But one senses that he wanted to be one with Feisal, Auda, Nasir and the rest, yet could not because he knew too well what had been planned, and that this inner leash of conscience holding him back from complete abandonment to the world of his companions was an agony to him.

It was at this time that he says he made a secret and doubtless dangerous journey to Damascus, its itinerary unknown and its purpose vague, the mystery surrounding it compounded by the elaborately elusive answers he later gave when questioned about it by Robert Graves. George Antonius, in *The Arab Awakening*, says that he 'went off alone on one of the most original and daring expeditions of his career', dynamiting as far to the north-west as Baalbek, then meeting Rida Pasha Rikabi, an Arab and subversive general in the Turkish army, giving him a message about Feisal's long-term intentions before spreading the same message among other Arab leaders far behind the Turkish lines; Lawrence later denied some of these details. He returned, in any case, on 16 June, and three days later the expedition to take Akaba set out. It was some five hundred strong, confident, well armed, its camels strong and swift and fresh. Auda had sufficient certainty to suggest that Lawrence 'get him a worthy gift from Feisal when he won Akaba'. But they discovered at Bair that wells they were hoping to use had been blown up and this brought them up in perplexity; perhaps the Turks were after all ahead of them.

By deliberately lost documents and other stratagems it had been hoped to persuade the Turks that the target of any new Sherifiate thrust would be towards Damascus; now Lawrence thought this suggestion might be reinforced by direct action. With 110 men, he and Auda's nephew, Zaal, rode northwards for a hundred miles, covering the distance in thirty-six hours, and struck at the Hejaz Railway not far from Deraa. Forty miles south of Amman, when they were already on their way back, they took the small Turkish garrison at Atwi by surprise, blew up more rails, killed such Turks as they could reach and plundered what was open to them – then had to spend three hours chasing their panicked camels and a herd of plundered sheep.

During the week of this diversionary journey, the main force had been supplied with enough flour for the whole march west-ward to Akaba. The blown-up wells at Bair had sensibly made Auda and Nasir suspicious; it was decided to send a party ahead to take and hold the wells at Aba el Lissan. By doing this, however, other Turkish units in the neighbourhood were put on the alert. Aba el Lissan lay at the foot of the last mountain ridge on the way to the Red Sea and the road to it wound through a valley; by the time the main body of Howeitat reached it, a Turkish battalion, supported by artillery, had been deployed to hold it. Their position would have been almost impregnable had they not been too careless to post scouts and look-outs; clambering cautiously through the broken ground and across the long, dun-brown slopes, the Arab force managed to get above them. The Turkish position, however, was too well-established, too well-protected by an impartial Nature, to permit Auda's force to turn it even from the high ground. So through the spiralling heat the bullets hissed or howled off rock, the high-explosive shells flung their jagged rain across the valley, the hammer-blows of artillery fire and the sharper rattle of the rifles smacked and echoed about the unappeal-ing slopes. It was at this point of stalemate, according to Lawrence, that Auda, a man given to weaving his own exploits and those of his men into complex sagas of heroism, and who had been teased for his boasting by Lawrence, cried out to him, his voice harsh with frustration, 'Well, how is it with the Howeitat? All talk and no work?'

Lawrence himself was in no mood for politeness. 'By God, indeed,' he spat, 'they shoot a lot and hit a little.'

Auda, furious, threw down his head-dress and rallied his men. 'Get your camel if you want to see the old man's work,' he said, with a contained fierceness. And as Lawrence and Nasir mounted their camels, he disappeared, to emerge again in the valley below at the head of fifty yelling horsemen, who, shooting from the hip, careered down upon the hapless Turks. As these, so ferociously assaulted, wavered and broke, Nasir gave his own order and, with Lawrence at his side and four hundred camel-mounted men behind him, came racing down the slope to take the Turks in the flank.

Arab troops in training at
Akaba in 1917.

122

Sherifiate leaders in Wadi Itm, discussing possible terms for a Turkish surrender at Akaba. It was decided to send the garrison there a message under a flag of truce inviting their surrender. But all efforts to agree to a parley failed.

Terrified, overtaken, brushed aside, the Turks scattered, then ran. Lawrence, pistol blasting, raced among them. And suddenly the world gave way beneath him – his camel dropped in mid-stride. He fell hugely and lay stunned, to come to into silence, the battle over and victory won. When he looked to see what had happened to his mount, Naama, the Sherari racing camel, he found that in his excitement he had shot her through the back of the head.

Then there was plunder, and interrogation of prisoners. This last was tough – Lawrence tells of taking one and 'shocking him by new pain into a half-understanding', a phrase which sits oddly so close to a meditative passage on the Turkish killed: 'The dead men looked wonderfully beautiful. The night was shining gently down, softening them into new ivory. . . . Surely if straightened they would be comfortable at last. So I put them all in order, one by one. . . .' But the war would not wait upon philosophy. Messages were sent to neighbouring tribes, spreading word of the victory and urging them to take Turkish units prisoner in their own areas. A Turkish officer was persuaded to write letters to other garrisons along the route, urging their surrender. Then, before sun-up, they were on the move once more, to find that success had eased their path – everywhere Turkish units had either retreated or been taken, and everywhere more tribesmen, happy in the hope of loot and avid for a chance of hitting at their masters, came riding out of the scrub-covered landscape to join their force.

Akaba, they learned, was held by not more than three hundred Turks. They were short of supplies, but were expected to fight. In Wadi Itm, a few miles from their objective, Auda, Nasir and Lawrence stopped to discuss what they should do. 'Arguments bickered between the prudent and the bold,' Lawrence writes, but he wanted no unnecessary bloodshed, although all around him the pressure for violence was building up behind a thin dam of discipline. Two messages were sent to the Turks; their reply each time was rifle fire. A retributive assault almost began then and there, and only Nasir held the Arabs back. A Turkish prisoner was sent in with a third message, and he got through. He came back an hour later with a reply: if no help came for them, the garrison would surrender in two days. It was too long; a parley was arranged, and the position explained to the Turks – the Arab force was growing all the time, no power on earth could hold them back another forty-eight hours. It was surrender soon or take the consequence of battle. The Turks saw the logic of this and agreed to lay down their arms at dawn. There was another outbreak of

The Taking of Akaba

Akaba, held by the Turks, was vital to the Arabs because it gave them an entry to the Red Sea. The final sweep into the town did not end until it reached the water's edge, where Lawrence and Auda expressed their delight by paddling in the waves.

ABOVE Representatives of the assembled local tribes coming to swear allegiance to Feisal at Akaba.
BELOW The triumphal entry of the Arab column into Akaba on 6 July 1917.

Nuri es Said, Chief of Jaafar
Pasha's staff, commanding
troops at Akaba. Jaafar
Pasha had joined the
Arabs at Wejh.

The ruins of the fort at Akaba.

firing just before the appointed time, but Nasir marched his men towards the town in such parade-ground order that everyone could see there was to be no battle. On 6 July 1917, two months after Nasir, Lawrence and Auda had left Feisal at Wejh, they were rushing through the streets of Akaba, grey under wind-driven sand, to leap at last into the easy waves of the Red Sea's long arm.

Brémond was to write, and Aldington to copy him, that this taking of Akaba was no great feat, since it had already been done twice before in that war, by French and British sea-borne detachments. But those had been raids; coming in from the sea, these units had been vulnerable to the Turkish forces still on the overlooking hills and could not consolidate their positions. To take that high ground would have meant for them an operation like a smaller version of the Dardanelles battle. Lawrence seems to have been the man who conceived the long detour to the east, the swift rush westward, the unexpected attack from the unexpected quarter. He had set out under Nasir's leadership with Auda and less than forty riders, had travelled some eight hundred miles, arriving at last with more than a thousand men and, without Allied help and in the sole name of the Sherifiate, had taken this crucial port.

4
Games
of War and Death

I am staying here a few days; resting my camels, and then will have another fling. Last 'fling' was two railway engines. One burst into fragments, & the other fell on the first. Quite a successful moment! If you see a note in print saying that 'A detachment of the N. army of Sherif Feisal etc.' Then that's me . . . the rest is anonymous.

To his family, from Azrak, 14 November 1917

IN AKABA, FOOD AND SUPPLIES WERE LOW, buildings lay in ruins after the previous assaults, there was no communication possible with Cairo. Lawrence had his triumph, but the world did not know of it; more, it was threatened, for if no supplies were sent in, the force he had helped to raise would melt away. Leaving Auda to set up a defensive network based on Guweira and Petra, Lawrence set off for Suez. After two months of travel, negotiation, tension and bloodshed, he found the strength and stamina to cover the 150 miles in just over two full days. With his eight companions he reached Shatt, opposite Suez, on the afternoon of 9 July, to find it deserted. He unearthed a telephone, called Suez and asked to be ferried across. Met by bland evasions of responsibility, referred here, then there, he became vehement, was cut off, to be finally rescued by the intervention of the operator: 'It's no bluidy good, sir, talkin to them fookin water boogers,' he said, and connected him to Major Lyttleton, the embarkation officer, a man in sympathy with the Arab Revolt.

Across on the African side of the water and on a train for Cairo, he met with further problems – the military police appeared, their harvest those travelling without passes. Lawrence brought them to a halt. What unit was he from? 'Sherif of Mecca – Staff.' The police were baffled. 'They looked at my bare feet, white silk robes and gold head-rope and dagger.' They had never heard of a Meccan army, did not recognize his uniform. 'Would you recognize a Montenegrin dragoon?' Lawrence asked. There were too many armies, too many uniforms; they let him travel on. (Another version of this story sets it on Ismailia station, Lawrence's interrogator a staff officer and his actually the line, 'What are you? A bloody Montenegrin dragoon?' In that tale, too, Lawrence ends on top. 'Meccan army?' bellows the officer. 'Never heard of it!' Lawrence replies, quietly, 'You will very soon.')

It was, one way or the other, on Ismalia station that he finally was able to give his message to authority, for Admiral Wemyss was there, conferring between trains with a khaki-clad group bright with the red tabs of staff officers. Was it Wemyss who saw him and remembered him, as one story insists, or was it a naval flag-captain, Burmester, whom he accosted? It hardly matters now. HMS *Dufferin* was given the task of ferrying supplies to Akaba, and laden with food and stores and sixteen thousand gold coins, reached that bedraggled port on 13 July. But that day at Ismalia Lawrence learned something of importance himself. Burmester had taken on the responsibility for re-routing the *Dufferin*,

PREVIOUS PAGES Lawrence's main supply depot in Akaba. At the time of its capture, the town's inhabitants were starving. Food supplies had to be organized for them and for the Arab forces which had made the entry. Streets in ruins from an Anglo-French naval bombardment and a complete lack of telegraphic or other communications with the main British forces contributed to the town's desperate condition. Lawrence made a dash to Cairo in order to bring news of Akaba's capture and subsequent flight.

OPPOSITE Lawrence on camelback at Akaba. His strategy at Akaba had been brilliant – by attacking the Turks from behind instead of from the sea, he had caught them unprepared.

for he did not want, he said, to disturb Admiral Wemyss's discussion with General Allenby. Lawrence was astonished. What was Allenby doing there?

'Oh,' Burmester told him. 'He's in command now.'

'And Murray?'

'Gone home.'

Lawrence was not unhappy at Murray's departure, but uncertain of this new commander. Would they 'have trouble for six months teaching him'? He was soon to discover for himself what sort of man Allenby was, for in Cairo the news of Lawrence's success at Akaba spread swiftly, and praise and honours followed on the news. He was promoted to major, he was awarded the French Croix de Guerre (Brémond wrote the relevant report), he was recommended for the Order of the Bath and would soon be given it. Clayton, overlooking Lawrence's cavalier circumvention of his orders, agreed to give all the assistance he could. And Allenby summoned him to a meeting. The vast Allenby, faced,

'Wind': a cartoon by Eric Kennington from *Seven Pillars of Wisdom*. It shows the scene at Ismailia station. Here Lawrence, bound for Cairo, encountered a party of military officials and discovered that General Allenby had been appointed to succeed Murray.

in Lawrence's own words, by 'a little bare-footed silk-skirted man . . . could not make out how much was genuine performer and how much charlatan'. Lawrence 'left him unhelped to solve it' and he probably never did; Wavell, in his biography of his fellow field-marshal, *Allenby: a Study in Greatness*, reports him as having always suspected Lawrence of bearing 'a strong streak of the charlatan' in him. But Allenby had the imagination and the courage to realize that if he was to use Lawrence at all, it would have to be on Lawrence's terms. He knew the terrain, he knew the people and he had been instrumental in taking Akaba; he welcomed responsibility and detested restraint – he was, in short, the ideal lieutenant for a commander prepared to delegate and not afraid of the unorthodox. Allenby may, indeed, have been sufficiently sensitive to realize that a man who, as he told the commander of the 4th Cavalry Division, General Barrow, 'loves posturing in the limelight' need not be less effective for such a weakness; he may in fact have a greater eagerness to succeed than more retiring souls. In any case, as he was to write later, he gave Lawrence a free hand; Lawrence in return gave him an extravagant and unfailing devotion.

Now, perhaps, his standing high with both commander-in-chief and staff, Lawrence might have brought to a climax the political dilemma which, he says, was beginning to torture him. He might have demanded some final clarification of Allied intentions towards the Arabs, some statement which would have counterweighted or even undermined the Sykes-Picot agreement. Failing that, he might have demanded his own transfer from an impossible situation. He did neither. He asked for a freer hand, with independence from Joyce and Newcombe, he proposed an integration between Allenby's Egyptian Expeditionary Force and Feisal's army, he suggested that Feisal should make his headquarters in Akaba, and so become the right wing of the Allied armies. And most of what he asked for, Allenby endorsed.

Soon Lawrence was back in Wejh, then Jiddah, busily arranging Feisal's move. The Arab force was nominally under Wingate's command, Wilson was Wingate's representative with the Sherifiate leadership, and upon whether he could be placated or persuaded hung success with Hussein. As it happened, all this diplomatic effort passed off without problems, but 'two abrupt telegrams from Egypt shattered our peace': Auda and his Howeitat were in double-dealing contact with the Turks at Maan. A dash by ship and camel, then confrontation at Guweira; the Howeitat

The room in which
Lawrence slept at Akaba.

leaders proved at once anxious and truculent, pointing out with some justice that they had received neither guns nor reward for their effort in Akaba. (Cairo's medals and acclaim had, after all, gone mostly to Lawrence.) Apparently relaxed, amused, but dropping into the conversation disturbing phrases taken from their intercepted correspondence, Lawrence pointed out that once Feisal was in Akaba, food, weapons and money would be sent there in great quantities. He offered Auda an advance on his share of these. He did not moralize – Auda remained in Feisal's train as long as self-interest dictated, and Lawrence accepted that. He laughed; the proposed defection became a joke between them; and so it passed off, the conclusion of the crisis yet another sheep killed to become the centre-piece of an amicable feast.

Akaba, injected with Allied supplies, came to abrupt and teeming life. Within six weeks of its capture it had become a solidly

136

established base, fluttering with the robes of the Arab armies, harsh with the khaki of French and British troops. But at Maan the Turks were gathering, strengthening their garrison there with the cavalry of tradition and the bombers of the new technology, then sending a large detachment to hold Aba el Lissan, where one hopes the ghosts of their recently overrun comrades did not disturb them. They too were destined for sacrifice, for at Lawrence's request aircraft were based on Akaba and were soon flinging death at the Turks, both there and in Maan itself, their passing marked by memorial columns of dust and smoke.

And this period saw the beginning of the months during which Lawrence rode out on those expeditions which were the essence of his legend, then among the Arab tribesmen, later in the west. His objective was part political, part military, his method the swift raid on the Hejaz Railway. Of the two, the political was

A stretch of the Turkish Hejaz railway, between El Nijh and Shobek. Having taken Akaba, Lawrence now concentrated on sending out raiding parties to blow up the lines, telegraph poles and, occasionally, trains.

137

perhaps slightly the more important – tribes were drawing back from the Revolt, there were doubts about Feisal, suspicions that he was in the pockets of the Christian powers of Europe. Turkish agents whispered in tents and market-places, and some at least were able to cite the Sykes-Picot pact to underline British and French untrustworthiness. It was a time to strike, to demonstrate that power lay with Feisal and that the fruits of it would be shared with those who helped him.

Lawrence chose the station at Mudawara, eighty miles from Maan, as his target – 'A smashed train there would embarrass the enemy.' With two instructor sergeants to oversee the machine-gun and mortar sections (they were called 'Lewis' and 'Stokes' after the guns they tended), and with one of Feisal's officers, Sheikh Aid, a string of camels loaded with explosives and the men to see to them, he made his way towards Guweira. Almost at once there were problems. Aid was stricken by a sudden blindness. Many of the local Bedouins, rivals of Auda, were reluctant to help those who were Auda's friends, although their chief spokesman, Gasim abu Dumeik, had fought in the victory at Aba el Lissan. Lawrence settled to discussion. The sun beat and battered, the heat an enclosing prison; talk moved sluggishly. Only on the next day when Auda's nephew, Zaal, had arrived did the dialectical tide turn. Most of the sheikhs finally promised to support Feisal – if the Emir promised to underwrite their tribes' independence, most especially from Auda. With this proposal, Lawrence returned to Akaba, startling Feisal by his unexpected arrival. Soon he was back in Guweira, this time with one of Feisal's ablest mediators, and the delicately balanced treaty was at last agreed. It was therefore with a hundred of these new and slightly reluctant allies that Lawrence finally rode on to Mudawara. It was 16 September, his force only a third of what he had planned for.

As a result, the station itself proved too heavily defended, Lawrence's force too reduced to venture a frontal attack. He moved a few miles south, therefore, to where a small bridge overlooked by a little plateau made an ideal site for laying a mine, hoisting with it the next passing locomotive, then catching the derailed wreckage in a destructive cross-fire. The trap was set; the raiders settled down to wait for their victim. But the Arabs, according to Lawrence always contemptuous of the Turks, grew careless as they watched. Soon a Turkish force was leaving Mudawara to drive them off, a hundred men on foot marching reluctantly through the bitter noonday heat. A train followed,

138

hissing into its iron-clad leap for safety; its two locomotives thrust it powerfully towards the point of ambush, soldiers within discharging their weapons in a random display of nervous power. Lawrence raised his hand; by the exploder's plunger, a man watched him, the train now driving upon the bridge, the first locomotive upon it, then past, the second in place and the hand plummeting in signal – and the triumphant roar of dynamite, the great column of black destruction lifting a hundred feet above the track, 'shattering crashes and long, loud metallic clangings of ripped steel', a pause while silence rearranged itself; and then the second phase of the attack. The surviving Turks rallied, but mortar fire brought them into the light; there, the Lewis guns cut them down as they ran. So the looting started, part of the reward which kept these volatile raiders in the tenuous control of their leaders: 'The Arabs, gone raving mad, were rushing about at top speed, bareheaded and half-naked, screaming, shooting into the air, clawing one another nail and fist, while they burst open trucks and staggered back and forward with immense bales. . . . There were scores of carpets spread about; dozens of mattresses and flowered quilts, blankets in heaps, clothes for men and women in full variety; clocks, cooking-pots, food, ornaments and weapons.' There were prisoners, too, but some were killed when a dispute broke out between them and Lawrence's excitable bodyguard. Laden, the Arabs departed; they had what they had come for. Only Zaal with one companion came back to look for Lawrence and for the two sergeants. All the while the force of Turkish infantry had been coming closer. Lewis and Zaal built a dangerous bonfire of the ammunition they now did not have the camels to carry; as a torrent of blasting broke out and bullets were flung like fireworks across the crackling air, the Turks halted; to their ears, a sizeable force awaited them. Covered, Lawrence and the rest made their escape.

In mid-September he wrote to a friend, 'The last stunt has been a few days on the Hejaz Railway, in which I potted a train with two engines (oh, the Gods were kind) and we killed superior numbers, and I got a good Baluch prayer rug and lost all my kit, and nearly my little self.' But the lively tone flags: 'I'm not going to last out this game much longer: nerves going and temper wearing thin, and one wants an unlimited account of both. . . . This killing and killing of Turks is horrible. When you charge in at the finish and find them all over the place in bits, and still alive many of them, and know that you have done hundreds in the same way before and must do hundreds more if you can.' It is no wonder that he hoped 'when this nightmare ends that I will wake up and become alive again.'

But it was not to end now. The Arab Revolt, since Akaba more smoke than flames, had been kindled once again. Now he became more and more the Lawrence legend gives, the small man, red-brown, his white robes fluttering in the wind of his advance, the brightness of his guard about him, the dust rising as they gallop through the endless curse of the heat, the long loops of their journeys hung on tall pillars of smoke, of debris, of flesh; then the brittle conversation of the guns and at last the silence pressing in like the palms of gigantic hands, the blood dark on the sand, the high whining of the gathering flies. . . . Again and again the Turks sallied from Medina to mend the fragile metal on which they depended; it was their good fortune that material to extend the railway had been stockpiled there. But they could not withdraw, they could not venture out, and as Lawrence and the rest, French and British, scattered the rolling stock unit by unit on the dark wings of dynamite, even their main armies began to find the movement of supplies restricted.

By mid-October, with Allenby's plans well-advanced for the coming assault on Jerusalem, the Commander-in-Chief summoned Lawrence to another interview. There is no doubt that Lawrence felt he had done rather well over the preceding weeks, but Allenby was brusque. 'He asked what our railway efforts meant,' Lawrence wrote in *Seven Pillars of Wisdom*; 'or rather if they meant anything beyond the melodramatic advertisement they gave to Feisal's cause.' It is clear that he had seen through to some of Lawrence's motivation, to the dilemma it caused this eccentric officer, and that he had little patience with it. Fortunately, he had more patience for the man. But Lawrence, agonizing later, wrote, 'Not for the first or last time service to two masters irked me.' It was his British master who now wanted to know what Lawrence could persuade the Arabs to do for him in the coming battle. Allenby would have liked an uprising, a nationalistic and committed wave sweeping into and through Deraa; the local leader there, Sheikh Talal el Hareidhin, was pleading to be allowed to give that crucial township to Lawrence, the Revolt and the cause of Turkish defeat. But Lawrence hesitated. What if the rising succeeded but the advance did not? What if the Arabs took Deraa but the Turks held Allenby? 'They could only rise once' – defeated then, they would be smashed for ever. And isolated by

140

British failure, they would be defeated. So Lawrence 'decided to postpone the hazards for the Arabs' sake'. It was also for Feisal's sake, for if Feisal was to be a king, it was he who would have to win the victories. Thus Lawrence broke faith with one master in order to keep faith with the other.

Since he had to do something to confirm Allenby's good opinion, however, he proposed what he later called the 'specious plan' of destroying the railway viaduct over the River Yarmuk. This carried the railway over an uncompromising gorge so deep as to make repairs both hazardous and lengthy. Since it lay beyond Deraa, halfway to the Sea of Galilee, hundreds of miles of Turkish-

The first and largest girder bridge after entering Yarmuk Valley. Lawrence had tried unsuccessfully to destroy this bridge during his first ride through Syria, in June 1917. In subsequent raids, too, he failed.

141

controlled territory would have to be crossed to reach it. The reward would be a total breakdown in the Turkish supply route between the safe bases far to the north and the war front in Palestine. In a lengthy battle, it could be the decisive factor, and Allenby accepted it as a plan sufficiently ambitious to compensate for his lost uprising. He wanted the viaduct to fall, he said, in the first week in November.

From Feisal, Lawrence borrowed one of his most spectacular henchmen, Ali ibn el Hussein, an adventurer whose fame was almost as widely broadcast as that of Auda himself, a man not only heroic in his exploits and his herculean strength – he could kneel down and, in Lawrence's words, 'rise to his feet with a man on each hand' – but also a relative of the Beni Sakhr, whose lands lay on the line of march. Persuading a tribe to friendship and assistance could of course be crucial when a raiding party ranged so far behind the Turkish lines, and the problem of doing so worried Lawrence. It was for this reason that he also welcomed the Algerian Emir Abd el Kader el Jazairi.

Lawrence knew that he could probably get help from the Serahin, who held lands around Azrak, some 250 miles from Akaba, and that he might be able to establish a base among them. But who would help him when he had penetrated the extra 150 miles to the Yarmuk? Now Abd el Kader brought the answer, for there were villages full of Algerian exiles living at Wadi Khalid on the north bank of that river. Abd el Kader himself came from a family with a long record of nationalistic resistance, against the French in Algeria before their exile, against the Turks since. When he said he could pledge the exiles' assistance, Lawrence believed him; when Brémond cabled a warning that he was not to be trusted, Lawrence disregarded it.

There were problems almost at once. Ali, the heroic figure, welcomed everywhere for his fame, aroused Abd el Kader's jealousy. Indian machine-gunners, taken along for a little militarily orthodox stiffening, found the camels too much for them. The British explosives specialist, Wood, fell ill with dysentery and the after-effects of a head-wound. When they stopped at old Auda's camp, they found that warrior so embroiled in his own endless quarrels that he could not travel with them; worse, while embracing Lawrence at parting, he too whispered, 'Beware of Abd el Kader.' But the welcome of the Beni Sakhr – 'wild cheers and gallopings and curvettings, and much firing of shots and shouting' – eased some of Lawrence's increasing despair. Only Abd el

142

Kader's ineffectual attempts to vie as a centre of attention with Ali, the Beni Sakhr's renowed kinsman, and 'Aurans, harbinger of action', brought a sour note to the celebration.

Next day they travelled on towards Azrak, with twenty of the Beni Sakhr now a part of their expedition. On the march, two famous warriors, the Sheikhs Adhub and Fahad of the Zebn Sukhur, also joined them. And, near Azrak itself, they met a party of the Serahin, led by their ancient Paramount Sheikh, Mteir, actually on their way to join Feisal and the Arab Revolt. Now, Lawrence thought, he would be assured of the guides and extra manpower he needed for the last dash northwards. But Mteir, though toothless, proved stubborn, and he was energetically supported by his younger battle commander – having heard the plan, nothing would induce them to take part. Turkish military wood-cutters filled the country and it would be impossible to make the journey without being seen. They also 'professed great suspicion of the Moorish villages, and of Abd el Kader'. As for the second bridge over the Yarmuk at Tel el Shehab, the villagers there were their enemies. So argument began, Lawrence bringing forward all his Arab companions to exercise their logic of pride, contempt and necessity, until the Serahin chiefs, persuaded by shame, agreed reluctantly to take part.

The British offensive had already been under way for five days; at intervals as they had travelled, the dull growling of the distant guns had come to them across the bleak, deserted miles and given them hope. (But 'I see no reason for gladness,' Abd el Kader had muttered to Ali. 'These are fellow Muslims caught in the deadly rain of the infidel's guns.') It was necessary to move quickly, however, so that by the next morning this divided and uncertain party was once more on its way. But a new disaster soon shocked them – 'When we turned again to business there was no Abd el Kader.' It was clear that this recalcitrant Algerian had defected and was on his way to warn those who had all along been his masters, the Turks. Nevertheless, Lawrence and Ali decided to push on – if they moved quickly, they could strike before the Turks were ready in defence. But strike where? Without Algerian co-operation, Wadi Khalid became impregnable; it was decided to make for Tel el Shehab.

They had thirteen hours before the next day's dawn, and eighty miles to cover. With his best men mounted on the swiftest camels, but with misgivings in his heart, Lawrence drove forward, hiding from patrols, struggling uncomfortably through drizzling rain,

143

ABOVE One of the British railway
raiding parties: Colonel Newcombe
stands on the left and Lieutenant
Hornby on the right.

OPPOSITE Another of Kennington's cartoons from *Seven Pillars*:
here Lawrence realizes that he is in full view of the
Turkish troops on the passing train he is trying to blow up,
and pretends to be 'a casual Bedouin'.

until 'from a lip of blackness rose very loudly the rushing of the river. . . . It was the edge of the Yarmuk gorge, and the bridge lay just under us to the right.' There had been no alarm here. Orders were whispered, the party divided: soon Lawrence, Ali and Fahad, followed by men carrying the necessary explosives, were crawling through the rain-swirl and darkness, until the metal of the bridge hung above them and, sixty yards away, they could see the slow pendulum march of the Turkish sentry. For a moment, all was silence, movement frozen, the world poised on the edge of action – and then disaster struck in the echoing clatter of a dropped rifle. The sentry, turning, saw the machine-gunners creeping through the moonlight to positions above him, challenged, fired. In a moment, surprise had turned against the raiders, the Turks were running into position, from the high hillsides there came the irregular flash of the Arabs' random fire; there could be no explosives set now. Lawrence dodged back through the Turkish bullets and gave the order to retreat.

The long return was gloomy. The Serahin robbed a party of peasants coming from Deraa and were left behind 'with their encumbering loot'. Quarrels broke out. When the railway was reached, Lawrence, determined to achieve at least one act of war, laid a charge; it sat under the rails in ineffectual neutrality as the next Turkish train ran over it. Lawrence remained exposed to full view as the Turks missed the expected disaster. Feebly, he waved to them as though no more than an innocent onlooker, to be accused

when they had gone of deliberately having spared the train. Fever-ridden but steadfast, Ali assured his companions that as a Sherif with the gift of second sight he knew their luck had changed. And sure enough, a little later another train came by, its main passenger the commander of the Turkish Eighth Army Corps, Jemal Pasha, on his way to face Allenby and try to hold Jerusalem.

The explosion halted it, comprehensively, but it also wounded Lawrence. Soon the Turks, rallying, began to reply to Arab fire, to push back the Arab attack. Lawrence, limping, looked as though he might be isolated. Ali led a rescue party of some twenty men; seven fell almost at once. The others reached him, to provide Lawrence, in *Seven Pillars of Wisdom*, with a paragraph about their appearance – 'fit models . . . for a sculptor . . . their slender waists and ankles, their hairless brown bodies' – which in the circumstances is so self-indulgently aesthetic as to imply a kind of contempt for his rescuers. But the battle still howled and crackled about him; the Turks had superior numbers and, as a commander-in-chief's escort, especial qualities of discipline and experience. They began to try to out-flank Lawrence's party. It was time to leave. Fahad, missing and thought killed, was stubbornly rescued by his fellow, Adhub; then the group, only some forty men now, were falling back on their camels, firing as they retreated, before · clambering on their beasts at last and racing off. 'Next day', Lawrence writes, 'we moved into Azrak, having a great welcome, and boasting – God forgive us – that we were victors.'

He knew very well the extent of his failure, however; Allenby had trusted him to deliver some stroke destructive of enemy morale and communications, and he had delivered nothing. With self-deceptive excuses, he skulked in Azrak; the rain, he insisted to himself, was bound to hold up Allenby and he would be better employed stoking the guttering flames of revolt among the Arabs than chasing up to headquarters to give Allenby bad news. He was wrong. The British offensive had struck at Turkish weakness near Beersheba, having deceived the enemy by drawing him to Gaza in the west. They stood on the edge of victory and if the Yarmuk viaduct had been broken behind the Turks, their guns might soon have sputtered into silence. The Palestine war would then have ended within days.

Lawrence, however, sat in Azrak, meeting Arab leaders from deep inside Syria, discovering day by day that their mood made all ready for a rising. He could, he realized, have organized that

146

The Somme campaign: dead soldiers in Lonage Wood, 1916. Lawrence experienced
an entirely different type of warfare from those soldiers who fought
in the tragic conditions of the Western Front. However, he was not uninvolved
in that wholesale slaughter, for two of his brothers lost their lives there.

British troops moving up to the trenches at Hooge in October 1917. At this period, Lawrence was engaged in activities from Akaba.

collapse of Deraa which Allenby had wanted, had he had the boldness to attempt it. Despite these flutterings of conscience, however, he basked in the warmth of his friendship with Ali, in the respect and companionship of these men come hundreds of miles to seek and take counsel with him. Nevertheless, both war and revolution demanded action; he realized, he wrote, that he should 'use this wintry weather to explore the country lying round about Deraa'. And, as though in response to this intention, there appeared out of the rain one morning the man who would act as his guide, Sheikh Talal el Hareidhin of Tafas, a man outlawed by the Turks, and with a price on his head – not surprisingly,

148

given that reputation credited him with the killing of twenty-three Turks during the previous two years. Soon, Lawrence had put to him his plan to reconnoitre the Deraa area; delighted with it, he agreed to act as guide. Within a very short while, he and Lawrence, with two men to guard them, were riding northwards into the lands which Turkey still controlled.

5 An End of Dreams

For myself, I have been so violently uprooted and plunged so deeply into a job too big for me, that everything feels unreal. I have dropped everything I ever did, and live only as a thief of opportunity, snatching chances of the moment when and where I see them. . . . Anyway these years of detachment have cured me of any desire ever to do anything for myself. When they untie my bonds I will not find in me any spur to action. However, actually one never thinks of afterwards: the time from the beginning is like one of those dreams which seems to last for aeons, and then you wake up with a start, and find that it has left nothing in your mind. Only the different thing about this dream is that so many people do not wake up in this life again.

To V. W. Richards, 15 September 1918

WHAT REALLY HAPPENED IN DERAA? It is the point upon which Lawrence's later character turns, perhaps; the crucial moment of change and revelation. He was altered afterwards, everyone insists; yet some suspect that nothing happened, that the whole story was a fantasy. What Lawrence reports is that without Talal, who was too well-known to accompany him, he walked into Deraa, to be challenged almost at once by a Turkish patrol. Accused of being a deserter from the Ottoman forces, Lawrence said that he was Ahmed ibn Bagr, a Circassian from Kuneitra and thus exempt from military service (a point upon which he was apparently wrong). The sergeant disregarded these explanations and willy-nilly enrolled him. The others in his section tried to reassure Lawrence – life need not be bad, he might even get leave next day, 'if he fulfilled the Bey's pleasure this evening'. The Bey to be pleasured was the military governor, whom Lawrence calls Nahi Bey.

Soon after dark, he was dragged by three men – 'I cursed my littleness' – through railway sidings and deserted streets, to a detached house and upstairs into Nahi Bey's bedroom. There the Turkish commander tried at first to force him into acquiescence, then to wheedle and persuade. Finally, he called for assistance, making the man holding Lawrence 'tear my clothes away bit by bit, till I stood there stark naked'. When the Turkish commander approached, Lawrence like any threatened virgin smashed his knee into the other's groin. The Bey, having recovered, beat Lawrence with his slipper, bit him in the neck, kissed him, then, finally, cut him with the point of a bayonet – 'the blood wavered down my side in a thin stream, and dripped on to the front of my thighs.'

He was then taken outside to be beaten; he describes in detail the whip the soldiers brought, which was, he says, Circassian, its thongs

. . . of supple black hide, rounded, and tapering from the thickness of a thumb at the grip (which was wrapped in silver, with a knob inlaid in black designs), down to a hard point much finer than a pencil. . . . At the instant of each stroke a hard white mark like a railway, darkening slowly into crimson, leaped over my skin, and a bead of blood swelled up wherever two ridges crossed. . . . I writhed and twisted involuntarily, but was held so tightly that my struggles were quite useless.

He was, he says, afraid he might cry out in English, 'but as long as my will would rule my lips I used only Arabic. . . .' He collapsed on the floor, 'where I snuggled down, dazed, panting for breath but

PREVIOUS PAGES Emir Zeid, another of Hussein's sons, and Abdullah with captured 7·5 inch mountain guns at Tafileh in January 1918. Zeid held it with a diminished garrison, having banished Auda and his warriors to the desert after a dispute.

OPPOSITE Lawrence in his familiar white robes, Arab tents behind him.

152

ABOVE Azraq castle. This
oasis, about fifty miles to the
east of Amman, was used
as a base by Feisal.
RIGHT Sunset over the
pools at Azraq.

G. B. Shaw: a portrait by
Augustus John. The
admiration of this great
playwright and critic for
Lawrence was at first
somewhat tempered, and
it was his wife who
persuaded him to take
Seven Pillars of Wisdom
seriously.

vaguely comfortable'. The corporal in charge now began to kick
him: 'I remember smiling idly at him, for a delicious warmth,
probably sexual, was swelling through me: and then that he flung
up his arm and hacked with the full length of his whip into my
groin.' He felt himself almost at the point of death at this moment,
but there was more to experience. 'I next knew that I was being
dragged about by two men, each disputing over a leg as though to
split me apart: while a third astride my back rode me like a horse.'
But the soldiers had overdone their punishment; when the Turkish
commander saw the bruised and lacerated body of what he had

156

hoped would be a bed-companion, he had Lawrence dragged away.

Curiously, he was placed in a lean-to where there was a store of quilts, while in a room next door there hung a convenient suit of clothes. So, beaten, scarred, bleeding and buggered, Lawrence made his painful escape. In his wanderings through that appalling morning, he discovered the approach to Deraa he had gone there to seek. But if he brought this back, he left something else behind – some part of him had, he wrote, gone dead,

... leaving me maimed, imperfect, only half myself. It could not have been the defilement, for no one ever held the body in less honour than I did myself. Probably it had been the breaking of the spirit by that frenzied nerve-shattering pain which had degraded me to beast level when it made me grovel to it, and which has journeyed with me since, a fascination and terror and morbid desire, lascivious and vicious, perhaps, but like the striving of a moth towards its flame.

There are elements in this account which strike one as fantasy. That precise description of the Circassian whip, for example, its details seen so true and clear, apparently, when neither the appearance of men nor the furniture of rooms has been remembered with any precision. It reads like a masochistic day-dream. And what of the name 'ibn Bagr' – can one take that as one of Lawrence's bitterer jokes, a pun like Dylan Thomas's Llareggyb? Bernard Shaw recorded that Lawrence had told him this account of what happened was not true. Yet to Shaw's wife, Charlotte, he wrote, 'For fear of being hurt, or rather, to earn five minutes' respite from a pain which drove me mad, I gave away the only possession we are born into the world with – our bodily integrity.' He wrote that he held the body in no honour. Was it nevertheless the sexual assault which had so marred him? If so, what was its real occasion – for, as Knightley and Simpson reveal in their *The Secret Lives of Lawrence of Arabia*, Hacim Bey, the man Lawrence described as so desiring him (his name was changed to 'Nahi' for publication), was in fact a committed heterosexual with a varied and indiscriminate appetite for women, against whom not even his enemies ever levelled an accusation of homosexuality.

Lawrence was a man who often used truth as no more than a launching pad for fantasy, the fantasy then revealing inner truths mere factual veracity would have concealed. Hence, for example, his endless tales of humiliating senior officers who had not recognized his rank – at whom was he really striking, who was it who had not recognized him, whom did he desperately want to

157

prove his own inferior? These are the questions such fantasies raise (to which my answer, irrelevant here, would be the Chapman family, silent through the years of fame). Thus in the case of the torture at Deraa, one is tempted to inquire, if it did not happen exactly as Lawrence described it, what truth did his descriptions cover?

It is perhaps significant that in the later editions of *Seven Pillars of Wisdom* the passages describing his continuing fascination with pain were taken out. In other papers and accounts there is a strong suggestion that the Turks knew very well whom they had captured, that he had been betrayed by Abd el Kader and trapped deliberately (although in that event it is hard to believe he would have been let go). Thus arrested, he would certainly have been tortured. It is not impossible to believe that during that torture he was forced to recognize something his own picture of himself had hidden from him. As Anthony Nutting put it in his *Lawrence of Arabia: The Man – and the Motive*, he learned 'that he was no risen prophet, no Son of God, but a rabid masochist, whose happy endurance of pain disclosed a perversion of the flesh rather than a triumph of the spirit'. The very centre of his pride, that he could suffer without a murmur, that he could take punishment, the drawn-out agony of endurance, the endless ache of fatigue, better and for longer than other men, had been torn from him. More, despite his passionate friendships, despite his evident love for Dahoum, it seems likely that, in his relations with others, he 'had neither flesh nor carnality of any kind', as Vyvyan Richards told Knightley and Simpson. With his view of himself and his know-ledge of the Middle Ages, it is likely that he misconstrued this physical disability as a spiritual possession of great value, that he saw himself as an ascetic and so fit for dedication to a great cause. Seduced by pain into an undeniable pleasure, he would see this version of himself too as a self-deceiving idealization bitterly mocked by the reality.

Whether it was something of this sort that altered him, or whether strain and sickness, time and effort, had at last consumed the dedication which fuelled his spirit, he seems to have changed after his return from Deraa. He became less boyish, less easily swept along by present events, a harder man, sometimes harsh with those around him, often harsh about himself. It was in this desolate mood that he rode back to Akaba, the journey brutal and carried on at the very limits of endurance. One cannot help feeling that one of his objectives might now have been to confirm his

158

Charlotte Shaw,
photographed at her home
in London in 1905. She was
perhaps the only woman
Lawrence was ever close to.

detestation of himself through the criticisms with which Allenby
– the unquestioned leader, the disguised father-figure – would
punish him for his failure at Yarmuk.

Instead, when Lawrence had travelled by aircraft to Suez and
on to Allenby's headquarters near Gaza, he found the general too
successful, perhaps, and almost certainly too shrewd, to use the
sharp words a less imaginative commander would have reached
for. Instead, though probably with some inner misgivings, he
continued his support for Lawrence and his unpredictable activities. On 9 December Jerusalem fell to Allied armies moving too fast
for the German and Turkish reserves to come to the city's defence.

159

In the celebratory procession which marked Allenby's entry into that ancient stone and mud-brick complex of intrigue and religion, Picot, the French representative, the same Georges Picot who had agreed with Sykes, marched beside General Clayton, 'with Major T. E. Lawrence as staff officer and Lieut.-Colonel W. H. Deedes, G.S.O.1 Intelligence . . .', to quote one of Lawrence's infrequent appearances in the official records.

The war, however, was by no means over, and Allenby decided that Feisal's forces should move north to the Dead Sea in order to attack the Turkish supply route to Jericho, the Allied army's next objective. After that, they should link up with the British right flank. His only insistence, overriding all Lawrence's objections, was that in order to be fully effective, the Arabs had to be taught Western methods of fighting in formation; he sent Colonel (later General) Dawnay to Akaba to see that this systematic approach to warfare was properly inculcated. Lawrence's rejoinder was to increase his bodyguard to ninety men, a band of well-mounted, slightly over-dressed, swaggering and consciously handsome fighters, practised, ruthless and confident. Thus his legendary status was given yet more support. S. C. Rolls, who served with the armoured cars recently arrived in Akaba, tells of driving Lawrence to Guweira, where Feisal had set up his headquarters. 'We were met by expert horsemen who rode bare-backed, like fury, round and round, firing rifles in the air and yelling "Aurans! Aurans!"' But Feisal was not the leader Lawrence had thought him – which may mean no more than that he was beginning to have his own doubts about Lawrence. 'On our long rides T. E. often confided his difficulties to me,' Rolls recalled, 'his efforts to persuade Feisal who was continually losing heart and had to be coaxed and encouraged. . . . I have time and time again had to return, in some instances 500 miles or more, to get gold, the all-powerful persuader.' So detachments were gathered and lashed, argued or bought into battle; one senses that Arabs were beginning to ask with more and more pertinacity whether the war they were fighting was really the same as that which preoccupied the British.

To reach the Dead Sea, it was necessary to capture Tafileh, and so open the southern approaches to that bitter water. A three-pronged attack was decided on. The eastern column, under Sherif Nasir and Nuri es Said (to be many times Prime Minister of Irak, until killed in the 1958 revolution), were soon able with the aid of a little luck to take the crucial railway station of Jurf, blocking the advance of any possible Turkish reinforcements. Now they were

160

'Kindergarten': a cartoon by
Kennington, from *Seven
Pillars*. Here Lawrence
is depicted trying to
persuade the British military
staff of the folly of spending
money on the attempt to
take Medina. His own view
was that Damascus should
be the major objective.

joined by an old colleague, Auda, and so strengthened marched
on, unconcerned about the other two attacking groups to the west
of them. Tafileh, however, was held not only by some two hundred
Turks, it also had a pro-Turkish garrison of its own villagers, in
feud with neighbours who sided with Feisal. Through the bullets
that met the attackers, however, a furious but stately Auda rode
with the unconcern of the outraged. 'Dogs, do you not know
Auda?' he yelled, a chieftain come to demand allegiance. Awed,
both Turks and locals laid down their arms. That evening Sherif
Zeid, Feisal's young brother, in charge of the march to the Dead
Sea, was able to ride safely into the captured village.

There were, however, the beginnings of a feud between two of
Zeid's followers and Auda's family; there had been a killing, now
there were accusations, the old warrior roaring contemptuous and

insulting refutations. Zeid had to intervene, his judgment a dismissal of Auda and his men – not the last mistake the Sherif was to make, nor the least, for Tafileh was now under-garrisoned. Thus when, nine days after the Arabs had taken it, the Turks massively counter-attacked, Zeid proposed withdrawal to defensive positions south of the ravine of Tafileh. This of course meant leaving the town; instantly all was confusion, with villagers desperate at being left unprotected from Turkish vengeance. They were ready to stand with the Sherifiate force and fight if it would stand with them. Lawrence, uncharacteristically truculent, persuaded Zeid to do precisely that.

To the north the peasantry from nearby villages were holding a crest against the Turkish thrust. Lawrence sent a machine-gun unit forward to support them, and thus heartened they drove the

A view of Tafileh in January 1918. Tafileh was a strategically important village on the way to Damascus.

Turks before them over two ridges and on to the main body of their troops. From then on it was war as any high command might understand it, with the machine-guns blazing, then light artillery, shrapnel bursting above the deeply scored slopes, the sharp metal flailing out of the sky, men calling as they fell, or cursing, or screaming a traditional defiance. Thirty men of the Jazi tribe, thirty villagers and Lawrence were caught on a bare knoll, the fire of some fifteen machine-guns concentrated upon them. A Turkish warplane came clattering ominously out of the north.

Those on foot retreated, those with horses stayed, held for a while to cover them; then galloped after. On a sixty-foot high ridge, the Arab force rallied. Slowly, as they halted the Turkish advance and stabilized this suddenly created front, reinforcements came to them, sent up by Zeid; finally Zeid himself appeared with more guns, more men and some two hundred villagers as auxiliaries. Now there was cautious movement east and west among the ridges, an outflanking of the Turkish positions, enfilading fire, 'a frontal attack of eighteen men, two Vickers and two large Hotchkiss', a blast of fire from the western flank wiping out the Turkish machine-gun nests, a swift mounted charge from the east, and the enemy had been chased 'back past their guns into the bed of Wadi Hassa'. The story was told crisply in Lawrence's report to *The Arab Bulletin*; it was perhaps his only textbook action, and for that very reason he apparently despised it. Yet as a result, the Turks' traffic across the Dead Sea lay vulnerable to attack.

Lawrence was not content to leave this theoretically the case; he wanted to demonstrate it. Seventy horsemen, Bedouin from Beersheba (Lawrence, to judge from *Seven Pillars of Wisdom*, not actually among them), rode through the night around the edge of the water and on the morning of 28 January came bursting through the uneasy light of a winter's dawn to strike at the little port of Kerak. Loaded lighters and an armed launch, all ready for the journey to help supply the defenders of Jericho, still lay sleepily at anchor in the bay. The sailors guarding them were overrun before properly awake; the ships were taken out into deep water and scuttled. On land, the military post was burned, the sixty men who had been there, most of them sailors, were marched back, prisoners of the triumphant Arabs. Thus notice was served on the Turks that the supply route to Jericho was closed – a fortnight earlier than Lawrence had promised Allenby it would be.

Snow lay on the mountains of Moab, making the Arabs' next

allotted task of linking with Allenby's armies north of the Dead
Sea too difficult to attempt. In Tafileh itself, bleak at five thousand
feet, there was discomfort, boredom, quarrelling. The money
allotted to them had been spent; Zeid was running short of persuasion. Through blizzard, high ground, bitter winds, Lawrence
made his determined way on his unsuitable camels to Guweira,
where Dawnay and Joyce now had their headquarters. Here too
all was despondency, the mood blacker than winter: Feisal had
tried conventional warfare, as prescribed by headquarters, had
attempted to take Mudawara and, despite the presence of a French
gun battery under Captain Pisani, had been almost contemptuously
flung back. For Lawrence, there was compensation in this defeat,
the unpalatable compensation of a man who can say, 'I told you
so.' His mood was lifted, however, when during his appalling
return journey through the flat sleet, lashed across the high ridges
by searing winds, he stopped above the pass at Aba el Lissan to
visit a detachment of Feisal's forces led by one of the Emir's most
competent and single-minded officers, Maulud el Mukhlus. These
men, bodies stung and spirits eroded by the ceaseless cold, nevertheless clung to their high observation posts above the mountain
pass and the Hejaz Railway, their watch indomitable and of the
highest importance.

A fall into icy water, a camel coaxed along at the edge of near-
collapse, the endless assaults of the harsh-edged wind; then
Tafileh and a great warmth of welcome, though more for the gold
– there had been no pay for weeks – than for its carrier. Lawrence
gave it to Zeid to distribute, but warned him to keep some back
for the operations which awaited them. The following day, not
only were the men contented with money in their saddle-bags,
weather conditions too seemed to be easing. Lawrence, with
Lieutenant Kirkbride, an Arab-speaking officer sent forward by
Deedes, the Intelligence colonel, on a reconnaissance and from
then on appropriated by Lawrence ('a boy in years, but ruthless in
action', as he described this new recruit), rode forward to see
whether the march to join Allenby would be possible after all; they
found it was. Lawrence hurried back to Zeid, full of plans for the
advance. 'Zeid stopped me: "But that will need a lot of money,"' –
and confessed 'rather shamefacedly' that the money had all gone.
Against the rules which had been laid down, he had paid men not
on active service – 'so much . . . to Dhiab, sheikh of Tafileh; so
much to the villagers; so much to the Jazi Howeitat; so much to the
Beni Sakhr'. The march had been sabotaged before it could begin –

164

165

The Entry of the Allies into Jerusalem in December 1917, painted by James McBey. This victory was Allenby's (centre) achievement. Lawrence marched a few rows back in this parade, the French representative, Georges Picot, ironically beside him.

mid-day
Jerusalem December 1917

Lawrence and his bodyguard,
cause of certain caustic
witticisms from other Arab
campaigners, at Akaba in the
summer of 1918.

as Nasir pointed out, Zeid was 'too young and shy to counter his dishonest, cowardly counsellors'.

And Lawrence, either because he had come to the end of his resources, or perhaps in order to force Zeid to give the money back, threw in his hand. Joyce arrived at Tafileh at this high point of dissension and offered to intervene with Feisal, but it was too late for that. Perhaps for a moment the dilemmas of Lawrence's life had become intolerable, perhaps the recalcitrance of the human material he had to work with had become unbearable, perhaps the tensions and hardships surrounding him had at last become too great to bear; in any case, with Joyce to look after his affairs in Tafileh, 'I was able . . . to set off, late that afternoon, for Beersheba, the quickest way to British Headquarters.'

But the High Command would have none of Lawrence's self-indulgent desire for 'the security of custom: to be conveyed; to pillow myself on duty and obedience: irresponsibility'. Nor were they too concerned that he was 'tired to death of free-will'. He wrote in *Seven Pillars of Wisdom*, 'In my last five actions I had been hit, and my body so dreaded further pain that now I had to force myself under fire . . . and frost and dirt had poisoned my hurts into a festering mass of sores.' Worse, he felt, was his

168

corrosive knowledge of how insubstantial were the promises which had led the Arabs to join their effort to the British. Nevertheless, when Allenby, elated by his own recent capture of Jericho and charged by the War Cabinet to 'repair the stalemate of the West', told him how much he would rely on his liaison with Feisal to shore up the British eastern flank during the projected drive on Damascus and Aleppo, Lawrence changed his mind: 'There was no escape for me. I must take up again my mantle of fraud in the East.'

Early in March 1918, Lawrence was back in Akaba, giving Feisal the news that camels, artillery, machine-guns and £300,000 in gold had been ear-marked for the Arab cause. Their excitement at this Allied munificence was somewhat dampened by the news that Zeid had lost Tafileh, but Lawrence was now taken up with the Sherifiate's new objective, Maan, and felt that Turkish action elsewhere only served helpfully to draw defenders away. There was heavy argument as to how Maan should be taken; Lawrence wanted the town sealed off and the garrison forced out to re-open communications, then to be cut down. Maulud, on the other hand, saw it almost as a matter of honour that the assault should be frontal and direct – precisely the kind of action Lawrence had

169

spent most of his time trying to avoid. When Feisal, out of pride as much as anything else, agreed to the direct attempt, Lawrence had to accept the decision, but it was in a mood of some despondency that he rode off to Atara, in the Beni Sakhr territories, to set up his forward base.

Despondency was not to end there, however. To the north-west, the British advanced confidently, they took the town of Salt, they took Amman, everything seemed to point to swift victory; then there was counter-attack, a blunting of advance, finally withdrawal: Amman fell to the Turks again, then Salt. There, Arabs who had welcomed the British were being publicly hanged by Jemal Pasha. With his old comrade Farraj, Lawrence travelled to Amman to see conditions for himself. The two of them were disguised as 'merry little women' from a nearby group of gypsies, three actual gipsy women travelling with them to add substance to their cover. The plan nearly back-fired, and they escaped only a few strides from rapturous capture by the avid and licentious soldiery. The foray achieved nothing, nor could it alter by one iota the dismal unwinding of defeat and even tragedy.

Exposed by Allenby's retreat, there was nothing left for the Sherifiate force but withdrawal, Lawrence's pride and credibility among the Arabs dented by the British reverses. But a new and personal blow would hit him harder. During their ride south, they ran across a small Turkish patrol. Lawrence ordered an out-flanking attack; only Farraj would have none of such caution. He rode straight at the Turkish position, halted, seemed to wait. Tensely, Death hovered, then struck swiftly as rifle fire. Farraj fell. His friend and lover, Daud, had died of cold several weeks before; weary of life, he had chosen this way of following him. When Lawrence reached him, he was still alive, but so badly wounded that he could not be moved. Because of what the Turks did to their Arab prisoners, those so hurt they could not travel were shot by their comrades; now it was Lawrence who had to shoot this handsome founder of his bodyguard, this mischievous but endlessly faithful follower. 'I waited a moment, and he said "Daud will be angry with you," the old smile coming back so strangely to this grey shrinking face. I replied, "Salute him from me." He returned the formal answer, "God will give you peace," and at last wearily closed his eyes.' In this way, Lawrence lost perhaps his last link with those days, so full of zest and optimism and unthinking ambition, when he had first set out in search of Feisal's crown.

170

Back with the main Arab body, Lawrence discovered that Maan was holding fast; the regular drive and discipline of orthodox battle was not for them. Maulud had been badly wounded in the thigh. Nuri es Said – 'perfectly dressed and gloved, smoking his briar pipe' – managed to reach Maan station, but had to relinquish it when Pisani's covering gunfire flagged for lack of ammunition. The railway, however, was most effectively broken, one success to weigh against despondency. There followed, too, a long-range sweep by the armoured cars, supported by an Arab force and Egyptian regulars, the whole led by Dawnay and accompanied by Lawrence. He makes fun of Dawnay's meticulous planning, especially for the first day's operation, but has to concede that the only blot upon it was that 'the Turks, ignorantly and in haste, surrendered ten minutes too soon'; by the end of the raid eighty miles of rail and seven stations were in Allied hands, thus ending once and for all the threat represented by the Medina garrison, now entirely cut off. On the other hand it remained intact, like those at Maan and Amman which still prevented any easy advance northwards by Feisal's forces.

Back in Jerusalem to discuss and apologize for this, and to discover from Allenby what moves were being planned, Lawrence was set back on his heels to discover staff officers congratulating themselves on finding a new set of Arab allies in the Beni Sakhr sheikhs around Salt. Twenty thousand men, he was told, were being raised by Sheikh Fahad; his vexation and jealousy, his fears of being undermined, turned to an ugly exultation when, relied on to help the British re-take Salt, the Beni Sakhr remained 'supine in their tents'. Never a man happy to take blame, he now used the British reverses to excuse his own, and as usual was not reticent with criticism, allowing considerations of neither hierarchy nor rank to silence him. It was perhaps as well that his patron was commander-in-chief; had Allenby been moved elsewhere, Lawrence's tale would have had a different ending.

Allenby, his army whittled away by the inordinate demands of the bloody battles in the West, remained calm and kept his confidence in Lawrence. He agreed to give Feisal's forces air cover to drive the Turks into the open. When Lawrence asked for two thousand camels of the partly disbanded Imperial Camel Brigade, and Sir Walter Campbell, the Quartermaster-General, proved, as Lawrence put it, 'costive', Allenby invited both men to dinner. Over the meal, he asked Lawrence what he wanted the camels for.

'To put a thousand men into Deraa any day you please.'

172

Allenby gravely shook his head at Sir Walter. 'Q, you lose,' he said. And Lawrence felt a surge of optimism – he had been granted 'the gift of absolute mobility. The Arabs could now win their war when and where they liked.'

Such euphoria did not long survive reality. Not that he was disappointed in his reception by Feisal, Auda and the rest when he returned with his news of support and, above all, the promise of so vast a cavalcade of camels; nor was there any slackening of the old effort against the railway, which kept Medina, Maan and Amman separated and potentially vulnerable. Indeed, it was precisely his successes which were to bring him face to face with the political facts of Feisal's situation. Lawrence had conceived a grand strategy for the Arab armies – a bottling up of the Turks in Maan, a by-passing drive through Deraa towards Damascus, a linking with the British in Jericho. From Allenby's point of view it would have the advantage of drawing troops away from his front just at the period in October during which he was planning to attack. From Feisal's point of view, the advantage would be his unfettered arrival in Damascus at the moment when the British had only just started their advance, for Lawrence knew that 'the "promises" on which the Arabs worked were worth what their armed strength would be when the moment of fulfilment came.'

The snag in all these calculations was lack of man-power; the only way to counter it, a transfer of the units commanded by Ali and Abdullah from Hussein's forces to Feisal's. Feisal naturally agreed, and wrote to his father; from the Sudan, Wingate gave his slightly tepid support. Allenby, whom Lawrence visited in Jerusalem, agreed as usual – but dashed Lawrence's most optimistic expectation by telling him that the arrival of Indian reinforcements had allowed him to put the date of his advance forward by several weeks; Feisal's army and the British would now be moving at the same time. The margin of days during which Feisal could establish himself had thus been drastically reduced. Worse, however, was to come – Hussein would not give permission for the transfer of troops to his son. In October 1916 Hussein had proclaimed himself *Malik* or King of Arabia, a title he based in part on the promises made him by McMahon, and it was with a disturbed and jaundiced eye that he regarded Feisal's manœuvres on the borders of Syria. Thus, when Lawrence came to Jiddah in order to reason with him, he withdrew petulantly into the religious fastnesses of Mecca.

Two months later, his mistrust, stirred perhaps by Abdullah and his French advisers, led him to the folly of ousting Feisal from

OPPOSITE A sketch of General Allenby by James McBey. Despite Lawrence's various setbacks and failures, Allenby did not lose faith in the Arab cause.

the command of the Northern Army. The man appointed, Jaafar Pasha el Askeri, had long proved his loyalty as Feisal's chief of staff; he offered to resign. Feisal instead sent a protest to his father, was abused and so himself resigned. Hussein appointed young Zeid, but realizing his own limitations, Zeid refused the post. Now all was turmoil, with mutiny and dissension to season it, and before Allenby's pressure had finally forced the old Sherif vitriolically to reverse his appointments, Lawrence's dream of a united people gathered under the firmly benevolent rule of Feisal had been obliterated as though by a dust-storm.

All this while, too, there were the journeys, the conferences, the plans and arguments which precede an army's advance. It was just after Mudawara had been captured once more, this time by the rump of the Imperial Camel Corps, its single remaining brigade under Colonel Buxton having been transferred from Sinai, that Dawnay arrived from Allenby, partly in order to spread the good news of this success, but more importantly to warn Feisal not to rush into Damascus without taking account of the rest of the battle. 'The British push was a chance,' he pointed out, and too much haste might isolate the Arabs beyond hope of help. Feisal, however, 'replied that he would try this autumn for Damascus, though the heavens fell, and if the British were not able to carry their share of the attack, he would save his own people by making separate peace with Turkey'. Feisal's correspondence with the Turks (partly through Mohammed Said, the brother of Abd el Kader), which Lawrence knew about, had been bland, evasive and intended for their disarray. Now, it seemed, he was beginning to take it seriously. For Lawrence, his *raison d'être* Feisal's British connection, this flirtation loomed like a warning of disaster.

At this point Lawrence may have been close to breakdown. His uncertainties had multiplied, besetting his brain as his body had been beset by his privations. He felt, as jargon would put it, alienated from the world he moved in. Feisal seemed an actor, and he himself another beside him. The cause he thought himself committed to had always, as he was well aware, been secretly undermined by the imperial burrowings of European politicians. Now he took long, desperate stock of himself; it was his thirtieth birthday, a time others have thought right for such appraisal, and he did not like what he was, or was becoming. He picked at faults as though they were boils, half-savouring the pain: his craving to be liked, his craving to be famous, his 'eagerness to overhear and oversee myself', his inability to make easy contact with the

174

175

world. 'To put my hand on a living thing was defilement; and it made me tremble if they touched me . . .' he wrote, and 'Always feelings and illusion were at war within me . . .', and 'I . . . took my pleasures and adventures downwards. There seemed a certainty in degradation. . . .' He considered Feisal 'a brave, weak, ignorant spirit' whom he served, he thought, out of pity – a curious conclusion. He mentions again his reverence for Allenby, then returns to himself – to his envy of others praised, his unconcern for praise of himself, the odd cast of his mind which made him no longer want what was in reach: 'There was a special attraction in beginnings . . . .' He considered his approach to others, his treatment of them 'as so many targets for intellectual ingenuity:

A sketch of the Sinai desert during World War I, by James McBey. It indicates the barrenness of some of the terrain in which Lawrence operated.

A sketch of Lawrence by
Augustus John, who made
many portraits of him.

until I could hardly tell my own self where the leg-pulling began
or ended'. And he concludes, 'Indeed, the truth was I did not like
the "myself" I could see and hear.'

One need not doubt this; yet he was fascinated by the Lawrence
others could see and hear. He lived, one always senses, through
the reflected impact of his personality on others. Perhaps he
waited all his life for the one uncompromising, all-embracing
declaration of love which would have made him whole, and which
he may have thought had come to him from Dahoum and so from
the Arabs of his artificial cause. But by then it would always have
been too late – it could have come only from whoever had denied

him during boyhood. Was that, conventionally, his mother, professing a rectitude she had betrayed? Or was it the Chapman family, silent in the obscurity from which his affable father had emerged?

Action, however, would not wait upon introspection; force was mustering in Azrak. Most of the heroes of the Arab Revolt, Feisal at their head, had gathered there. Armoured cars and two airplanes had arrived to support them, as had Pisani's French artillery detachment and the Egyptian Camel Corps under their *Bimbashi* or Captain, F. G. Peake. Even the Druses, implacable fighters for their own freedom, had come down from their hills; even the plump town-dwellers of Syria had left their thin comforts to take their chance of liberty and plunder. The Arab forces were now well and truly a part of Allenby's offensive, their success and success in the western sectors irretrievably hinged together. If Allenby was held while they had even partial success, they would have struggled their way into a trap from which nothing could extricate them. Yet Allenby's advance partly depended on their assault drawing Turkish troops away from the point of his attack. It was a finely balanced plan, too finely balanced to be comfortable.

In the midst of these keyed-up partisans, Lawrence remained distant. 'I was tired to death of these Arabs; petty incarnate semites. . . .' Nevertheless, he was soon at his favourite action, blasting into oblivion sections of the eighty-foot bridge over which ran the railway south from Deraa, then being almost caught on the return journey when his Rolls-Royce tender broke down – an accident which would not, of course, have afflicted the camels of the earlier period. Now his unconcern became reflected in his actions; almost openly he marched around Deraa in order to blow up the railway linking it with Damascus. He chose a point only six miles north of the town, and was perhaps saved by the fortune which guides the temporarily mad, for the Turks had thought the post there too near Deraa to need reinforcing. Pisani's mobile battery hammered at the small redoubt, then the Arabs followed murderously; in a moment, the railway lay open to demolition. Only the Turkish warplanes posed a threat – 'three two-seaters, and four scouts and an old, yellow-bellied Albatross'. Against this one British plane climbed in defence, whirled effectively to and fro for a while, luring the enemy from their primary task and giving the Sherifiate force peace, then came down in a forced landing. Meanwhile, through bombing in which he was slightly wounded, Lawrence pressed on to the Palestine Railway, the line to Haifa and the main supply route for the armies facing Allenby.

178

Linking with Nuri es Said, he took the station at Mezerib – 'Nuri walked forward gloved and sworded, to receive the surrender of the forty soldiers left alive.'

As a result of all these skirmishes, this luxury of explosions on the British right, Liman von Sanders, the German supposed to lend new determination to the Middle Eastern war-front, was deceived; a concentration of dummy tents in the Jordan Valley completed his bemusement. He sent reinforcements into Deraa; in order to keep them immobilized it remained only to smash that viaduct at Yarmuk which had once before both tempted and resisted Lawrence. The young sheikh of Tel el Shehab brought to Lawrence the captain in charge of the bridge – an Armenian with reasons of his own to hate the Turks. With his assistance, the viaduct could be taken and destroyed. At the crucial moment, however, a trainload of German reinforcements passed that way, found the captain not at his post and in swift retribution arrested him. Lawrence hesitated, on the brink of attacking the troop train, but settled for explosions in two places beyond Tel el Shehab.

Next day he moved to the south of Deraa again, passing through demolished Mezerib to where the railway bridge at Nisib spanned its valley. It was too well-defended by fire from the nearby station, however, for men with gelignite in their pockets to venture among bullets. Lawrence, investigating, found that the bridge's immediate guard had slipped away; covered by Nuri's artillery barrage he and his companions crept towards the arches and were soon busily setting explosives in position. He was determined to bring the bridge down, 'since we were going to live opposite it at Umtaiye'; soon, with a harrowing roar, 'the black air became sibilant with flying stones' and the great structure disappeared. Thus was Deraa isolated, rail traffic into or out of roadless Palestine halted and the Turkish armies opposite Allenby faced with the choice to fight or die. There was no viable line of retreat now open to them.

News came that Allenby had moved, had thrust suddenly and unexpectedly, smashing the Turkish armies which opposed him. Lawrence hurried to see him, to find 'the great man unmoved, except for the light in his eye'. He was planning to give the Turks no rest; three columns were to be flung at them, one to advance on Amman, another on Deraa, the third on Kuneitra. Nor would the second and third columns halt at these objectives, but would push on to converge on Damascus. The Arab forces were given the task of assisting this advance by harassing in particular the Turkish 4th Army; Lawrence asked for air cover, and immediately

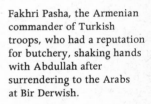

Fakhri Pasha, the Armenian commander of Turkish troops, who had a reputation for butchery, shaking hands with Abdullah after surrendering to the Arabs at Bir Derwish.

Some of Lawrence's wartime colleagues in the desert. Captain Hornby is in the centre, back to the camera.

obtained it, as well as air-lifted spares for the necessary fighters. (When the Handley-Page carrying the supplies had landed, the Arabs were awe-struck at its size compared with the scout-planes around it: 'Indeed and at last they have sent us THE aeroplane, of which these things were foals.')

Once again Deraa became the centre around which Arab detachments roamed to the punctuation of harsh explosions. There were four thousand men at this work now, and units could be spared to range northwards towards Damascus, returning with tales of Turkish demoralization and the unhappy prisoners to prove it. Finally the black smoke lifting over Deraa itself signalled the garrison's destruction of what could not be carried – they were preparing to retreat. Two thousand strong, their column reached northwards for safety. Only then did it strike Talal el Hareidhin, the sheikh of Tafas, that their route must be through his village and that his people lay vulnerable before the fury of their defeat. With Lawrence, he raced northwards to head them off. The move was too late. Jemal Pasha's regiment of lancers had already entered the village. As they marched out again, the Arab force attacked them – and Lawrence and Tallal rode into the village the Turks had just left. There was death, the hideous desolation of massacre, the piteousness of innocents overrun by a thoughtless, indiscriminate cruelty. Tallal, turning and screaming out his war-cry, rode to his death on the guns of the waiting Turks, but Auda, sitting harsh and grim beside Lawrence, said only, 'God give him mercy; we will take his price.' And so murder was enlarged, repeated and redoubled. 'In a madness born of the horror of Tafas we killed and killed, even blowing in the heads of the fallen and of the animals. . . .' Two hundred prisoners were shot down when one of Lawrence's own force was discovered, pinned and bleeding, on the ground.

At Deraa, Lawrence linked at last with a regular force, General Barrow's Indian Division. Barrow thought Lawrence an undisciplined and unreliable upstart; Lawrence thought the General a narrow-minded tyrant with neither the desire nor the ability to understand the Arabs. Both men were probably right. But Lawrence could now move up to Kiswe, a few miles short of Damascus, where Auda was resting after the slaughter, and where the Australian Division under General Chauvel was encamped and waiting for Barrow. There Lawrence, unnoticed, walked through the slow stir and murmur of the camp. He felt cut off from those he knew to be his own kin; he was, he thought, nearer to the Arabs than

182

to the troops, 'and I resented it, as shameful'. (Irreverently the thought intrudes that this mood was wilful, since a bath and a uniform would have altered his condition – but the drama was not yet run, and perhaps the melancholy was more bewitching than acceptance by his kind.)

In Damascus, at that very moment, the German and Turkish troops that had garrisoned it were marching out. As they left, Shukri el Ayubi, leader of Arab resistance in the city, ordered the raising of the Sherifiate's four-coloured flag; messengers hurried with the news to where Nasir, Lawrence, Auda, Nuri and the rest lay encamped.

At dawn, then, they finally rode into Damascus, Nasir in the lead, the veteran of fifty encounters, the battle commander, while the astounded crowd, struck into silence by their sudden liberty, stared bright-eyed at their saviours. Then, slowly, as they made their way through the city's narrow streets, a noise arose, the swelling roar of jubilation, the names of heroes endlessly repeated – 'Feisal! Nasir' and with them 'Aurans!' as the people broke free from stupefaction and crowded round their cars. For the moment, all seemed an ending filched from Lawrence's most ambitious dreams.

The reality was somewhat different. Even before the Arabs' entry on that 1 October, an Australian major named Olden had reached Damascus and it was to him that, anti-climactically, the surrender was made. Thus when Lawrence struggled at last into the unendurably crowded Town Hall, he found many notables already gathered there, deep in argumentative division of responsibility and spoils, prominent among them, to his horrified surprise, Abd el Kader and his fanatically religious brother, Mohammed Said. These, supported by their Moorish followers, presented the Sherifiate forces with an apparent *fait accompli* – they had assumed control of Damascus and would hold it in the name of the only King of the Arabs, Sherif Hussein. Lawrence, however, was the representative of both Allenby and Feisal and in their names he dissolved this council of usurpers and replaced it by a civil government headed by Shukri el Ayubi, but energized by Lawrence.

All now was strife, effort, struggle and improvised conciliation. Old Auda fought in the midst of the crowd with Sultan el Atrashe, a Druse chieftain known to have worked with the Turks. He had to be restrained from public murder, the Druse leader smuggled out of town. There was Chauvel and his brigade to re-route, argue with, then slot into place in the new scheme of things. There were the ambitious Algerians to put down a second time. And once some order had been established, there was all the mundane business of civilian administration to see to, so that there should be a functioning police force, lighted streets, sanitation, a water supply, justice, transport, a supervised currency, a postal service and above all, perhaps, a supply of food. To all these matters Lawrence gave his harassed but effective attention.

The next day, Abd el Kader and his force, supported by at least one group of Druses, broke out into open and, as they insisted, holy battle. But as against the Turks, the imperturbable tactical sense of Nuri es Said herded them to where machine-guns could manage them, and to the harsh laughter of the Hotchkiss this hasty revolt came to a bloody and ignominious end. Thus all was made quiet in the city for the ceremonial parade of Chauvel's army, the British, the French, the North Africans, the New Zealanders and Australians, the Indians, marching now as victors, the trained and disciplined professionals who had, for all Lawrence's fireworks and Nasir's leadership, Auda's dash and the quiet self-control of Nuri, been the real destroyers of the Turkish armies. 'A sideshow of a sideshow', Lawrence was to call his war, and one cannot meet the self-deprecatory appeal of this with any honest denial.

There remained a dash into the turmoil of the town, Kirkbride at his side, to prevent a massacre of the surviving Turks, and then his attempt to put into some sort of order the appalling military hospital, full of Turkish wounded, which he came across in a converted barracks: 'The stone floor was covered with dead bodies side by side . . . and they crept with rats, who had gnawed wet red galleries into them. . . . Inside the ward the air was raw and still, and the dressed batallion of filled beds so quiet that I thought these too were dead. . . .' Under Kirkbride, some of this horror was cleaned up by Turkish prisoners, the dead were buried, a few of the sick given at least the scant beginnings of care. The next day, a major in the Medical Corps stalked in, faced Lawrence with a brusque 'You're in charge?' before bursting out into a tirade – 'scandalous, disgraceful, outrageous, ought to be shot . . .'. And Lawrence, for whom this charnel-house had become perhaps a final commentary on his hopes, a final statement on the nature of the war he had fought, broke out into a wild, uncontrollable laughter, the hoarse cackling of hysteria.

And, indeed, it was a moment for such laughter. Allenby arrived in Damascus, and shortly after him, Feisal, the Emir upon

OPPOSITE, ABOVE
A Turkish train is blown up: a still from the popular film *Lawrence of Arabia*, in which Peter O'Toole starred as Lawrence.

BELOW *Turkish Transport Wrecked by Machine-gun Fire, Damascus 1918*. The painting is by James McBey.

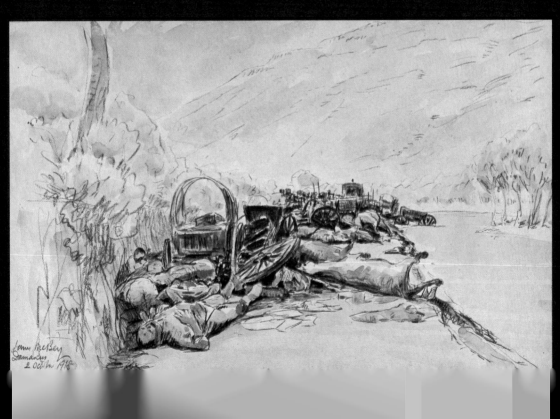

James McBey
Damascus
2 October 1918

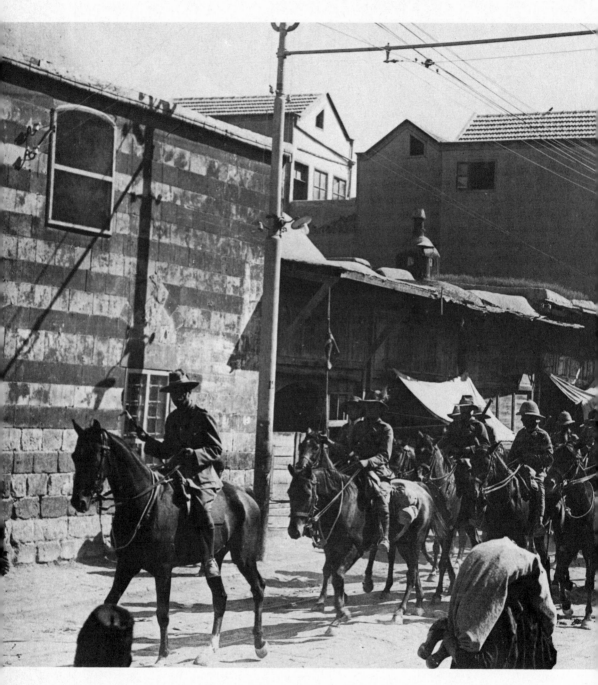

ABOVE General Chauvel rides through Damascus
on 2 October 1918. His bodyguard is a squadron
of the 2nd Light Horse Regiment. He led the
Australian division towards Damascus.

OPPOSITE 'A Literary Method': a cartoon by Kennington
from *Seven Pillars*, depicting Lawrence pinning like
an entomologist the many characters who had played
a part in the turbulent dramas of his war years.

whose slender shoulders Lawrence had once placed all his hopes, whom he had thought the man to build a kingdom in which an alien such as he might find honoured acceptance and a position from which to grimace contempt at the rejecting world outside. Now these hopes were over; and Feisal's with them. In the moment of triumph, Allenby with small preamble smashed the Emir's expectations on the rock, still half-concealed, of the Sykes-Picot agreement. France would be the protecting power in Syria. All the coastal lands west of the Jordan and along the Syrian littoral would be out of Feisal's jurisdiction; that would run from Akaba to Damascus – but as his father's representative only. Beirut, now in Sherifiate hands, would be surrendered. To help with the arrangements, a French and British liaison officer would be seconded to his staff. Feisal protested, but empires are built by force, and the force of Western Europe had not then run out.

Lawrence was to be the British liaison officer, his function to work shoulder-to-shoulder with a French colleague. It was more than he could bear. He was in any case at the end of his resources.

Always a man who lost interest in what he had gained, however hard he had struggled for it, his reaction now was the more extreme for the long struggle which had preceded it, and because after all so little had been gained – no kingdom for Feisal, no place for himself. He was weary, his sense of who he was, always perhaps shaky, had been undermined still further by his years of masquerade, the contradiction in his role which had so long troubled him had finally come to the moment of collision, perhaps the sheer administrative grind ahead – and with a Frenchman at his elbow! – was at once too dull and too daunting; in any case, he asked Allenby to release him and after a short wrangle, Allenby regretfully did. So within a few days Lawrence had reached and turned his back on the sad shards of his impossible kingdom.

OPPOSITE Richard Carline's painting of *Damascus and the Lebanon Mountains From 20,000 Feet, February 1920*. It gives a good aerial view of the region in which the Allies and Lawrence were planning their strategy.

6
Retreat from Legend

My own ambition is that the Arabs should be our first brown dominion, and not our last brown colony. Arabs react against you if you try to drive them, and they are as tenacious as Jews: but you can lead them without force anywhere, if nominally arm in arm.

To Lord Curzon in a memorandum, 27 September 1919

My losing the RAF numbs me, so that I haven't much feeling to spare for a while. In fact I find myself wishing all the time that my own curtain would fall. It seems as if I had finished, now.

To Peter Davies, 28 February 1935

IF IT IS TRUE THAT BY THE END OF THE WAR, Feisal considered that Lawrence, British and an infidel, had become an embarrassment and even an encumbrance, Lawrence felt differently about Feisal. One has to remember his idealization of the years of medieval chivalry, and to recognize that as a result Lawrence had a strong feeling for justice. And he felt very strongly that, quite apart from his own hopes, justice had not been done to Feisal. Back in Britain, he began a struggle to rectify this. Thus one finds him proposing to the Cabinet the creation of three states, to be ruled by Hussein's three sons, Feisal, Zeid and Abdullah; the embittered father, then deep in the wrangle with the Wahabi Ibn Saud which would lose him even what he held, would be confirmed as king of the Hejaz.

Meanwhile the French had moved into Lebanon and were beginning to crowd upon Feisal in Damascus. Uncertain of British support, he came to Europe to discuss the question with the British Government. When he came ashore at Marseilles, Lawrence, white-robed, was there to meet him. The French, however, Brémond their spearhead, objected to this Anglo-Arab, and Feisal

PREVIOUS PAGES Clouds Hill Cottage, Dorset, which Lawrence rented during the years that he was in the RAF, seen from the rhododendron wood.

BELOW Lawrence (second from right) with Feisal (third from right). In the foreground on the right, with his back to the camera, stands Lowell Thomas, the American who was to give Lawrence so much publicity.

Chaim Weizmann, the Zionist national leader who became the first president of the newly constituted state of Israel. Lawrence admired Weizmann, as well as seeing the usefulness of Jewish support to the Arab cause, in shaking off French influence.

sent Lawrence home. Perhaps he thought a conciliatory approach to the French might prove useful; it was, in any case, only a fortnight later that, in mid-December, he arrived in England. There followed talks, discussions, official visits, an audience with George v, Lawrence, sometimes in European, sometimes in Arab dress, an ambiguous and almost ghostly figure at the Emir's shoulder (*déraciné* in robes, he outraged the Court).

Among other people, Feisal met Chaim Weizmann, the Zionist leader and later president of Israel, their conference secret and arranged by Lawrence. For Lawrence, Jewish aspirations were

The Arabian Commission to the Peace Conference at Versailles and its advisers. This photograph, taken in Paris on 22 January 1919, shows Feisal (centre), Lawrence (third from right), Captain Pisani (centre, back row), and Nuri es Said (second from left).

a lever to be used against the French, and although Feisal and Weizmann disagreed about the nature of the planned Jewish community – Arabs wanted no Jewish state, Jews wanted nothing less – an agreement, albeit shaky and with declared reservations, was signed between them on 3 January 1919. As Lawrence saw it, Zionist participation in the Middle East with Feisal's co-operation would make the Emir financially independent of the French, and so able to resist their pressures. It might also, quite incidentally, have altered the next fifty years of Middle Eastern history.

Later that month there began at Versailles the great Peace Conference at which the far-sighted statesmen of Europe laid the foundations of World War II. Despite attempts by both the French and his embittered father to keep him out, Feisal attended the discussions on the Middle East. Lawrence was beside him, his role more ambiguous than ever, since he was officially one of the Hejaz delegation, but at the same time acted covertly as adviser to the British Government (or some sections of it, at least – the India Office, still doggedly suspicious of Hashemite claims, was busy in Ibn Saud's support). There now began a struggle reminiscent of hungry dogs around a bone, with the well-fed beasts of Europe aggressively disputing the best portions, the Zionist terrier snapping up what morsels came its way, the United States ambling to and fro like a benevolent but ineffectual St Bernard – and Feisal manœuvring with lean agility, but doomed for lack of weight. So bitter did Lawrence feel now that he embarrassed George V at an investiture by refusing his Order of the Bath, saying he could not accept it when he might at some time in the future find himself fighting for the Arabs against the British: 'He left me holding the box in my hand,' complained the King. Meanwhile Ibn Saud's victories over the Sherifiate armies, led by Abdullah and despatched by Hussein to teach the Wahabis a lesson, did nothing to strengthen the Hashemite case at Versailles. Drawing back from hard decisions, however, the Conference set up a commission of enquiry to look into the whole question, and Feisal returned in forced optimism to Damascus. In the event, two earnest Americans were the only ones to visit Syria, their report disregarded as soon as written.

For Lawrence it must have seemed as though within and without the universe had become too brittle for survival. His dream of somehow reconciling his own inner contradictions through the paradoxes of his involvement in the struggle for Hashemite autonomy had almost vanished. Two of his brothers had died in

OPPOSITE *A Peace Conference at the Quai d'Orsay* by Sir William Orpen. Feisal is to be seen on the left. The three men in the centre are (left to right) President Wilson, the French Prime Minister Clemenceau and Lloyd George.

196

the war. His father, urbane, enthusiastic, lovable, died in this year; his mother left for China with her eldest son, Bob (there to work as a missionary for the next three decades). He had been given a fellowship at All Souls worth £200 a year, in order to set down a history of the Arab Revolt. His mind turning to the book he might now write, he decided to travel to Cairo and collect his papers.

Perhaps his inner despondency made him a Jonah. The decrepit Handley-Page in which he was travelling crashed in Centocelle in Italy. Its two pilots died. Lawrence himself, clambering out of the wreckage with cracked ribs and a broken collar-bone, was soon travelling on in another aircraft. His presence in the Middle East caused nervousness in those who imagined he might take up arms against the French, but by August 1919 he was back in Britain.

The offical mood in London, meanwhile, had warmed to the French, cooled to Feisal. What moved the thermometer, then as so often since, was oil: an agreement which gave Britain oil-rich Mosul had as its price what the French called 'No dualism in Syria' – the unity, in other words, of French Beirut with Damascus. It was, in the end, an impossible choice of fighting or signing for Feisal; bitterly he initialled the papers which took away the independence he had spent three years of warfare to achieve.

For Lawrence, this was the proclamation of defeat. He had struggled through a desert of despondency, been dragged from one oasis of hope to the next; now he could see the full bleakness of betrayal. Ironically, it was at this moment that, like a genie unexpectedly released from some mundane and unsuspected receptacle, a spectre bearing his name but of improbable dimensions arose to mock him with a spurious fame. In 1917 an American, Lowell Thomas, had arrived in Palestine, charged with the task of making United States participation in the war more palatable by discovering for that country's volatile public a British hero they could take to their hearts. He had tried to do this in France and Flanders, but the boredom, the drabness, the butchery and the mud had defeated him. Transferring himself, with official approval, to the Middle East, he had stumbled on Lawrence and the romantic campaign among the sand-dunes and escarpments of a vaguely defined 'Arabia'. With, among other assistance, Lawrence's co-operation, he travelled a little about the country, he met Feisal, his photographer took a number of pictures, for some of which Lawrence, despite later disclaimers, most obligingly

The wreckage of the Handley-Page aircraft that crashed outside Rome in 1919, killing the pilots, Lieutenants Prince and Spratt. Lawrence was lucky to escape with injuries.

posed, and he listened to and wrote down a large number of tales, some of which were true, some of which were embroideries upon the truth and some of which were fictions. All this material he wove into a lecture, one of a set of five, which were, in the event, not to be given until after the Armistice. When he finally did give them, he discovered that it was this account of the Hejaz War and the drive on Damascus which really struck home to his audiences. When invited to England, he made the apparently impossible condition that he would come only if he were given the Theatre Royal, Drury Lane or the Royal Opera House, Covent Garden, to lecture in. In the event he got Covent Garden and on 14 August 1919, before an audience stiffened with starch and starry with diamonds, he launched the first of the series of lectures which,

ABOVE A portrait of
Lawrence as Aircraftman
Shaw, by Augustus John.
LEFT An RAF recruiting
poster designed by Norman
Keene, and issued in
March 1920.

over the years, would largely create that mythical figure, 'Lawrence of Arabia', part hero, part saint, the incarnate vindication of Empire, clean living and Anglo-Saxon supremacy.

In the Middle East, meanwhile, diplomatic intrigue was succeeded by the simpler processes of power politics. Feisal was summoned to the conference at San Remo at which all the area's problems were to be finally settled. He was in effect handed a map marked with the territories which would be controlled by Britain and France: Britain would have mandates over Palestine and Irak, and control over Mosul, France would have the Syrian mandate. An Arab congress meeting in Damascus had already confirmed Feisal as King of Syria and proclaimed his brother Abdullah as King of Irak, but no European statesman was prepared to take such nonsense seriously. Thus, when what are always known as 'extremists' took to the politics of the swift raid and the sudden explosion, the French moved. By the end of July, General Gouraud was in Damascus; Feisal's acceptance of French demands was ignored and he was ordered to leave for Palestine. Feisal had had enough – when the people of Damascus tried physically to prevent his departure, he ordered Nuri es Said's disciplined force to drive them back. By the beginning of next month he was in exile in Jerusalem, bitter, despondent, his cause once more a dream.

For Lawrence, the contradictions in his situation must have been almost unmanageable. Here were king and kingdom in disarray, while the would-be kingmaker was being hailed as someone combining the better qualities of Napoleon and Sir Galahad. Not only that, but one part of him, however much he had fallen under the sway of hard-edged Bedouin simplicity, had always been a calculating British political officer, determined to use that simplicity for his own patriotic ends. He had, in short, betrayed what he loved. Yet he permitted himself to be at least partly seduced by this suddenly released acclamation, went to Lowell Thomas's lectures (to remain, typically, in anonymity at the back), sat for numerous portraits and went to the galleries where they were exhibited, seized his new opportunities for meeting the mighty and the gifted, allowed himself to claim in *Who's Who* a title he knew could not exist: Prince of Mecca. Perhaps again Anthony Nutting has the answer when he writes, 'His sudden legendary status had helped his ego but it had not given him back his self-respect.'

Some semblance of this, however, was to be restored through

OVERLEAF Lowell Thomas, having successfully delivered his lectures on Lawrence in America, captivated English audiences at Covent Garden. Lawrence himself attended five or six times, with mixed feelings, alternately basking in and shrinking from the limelight: LEFT The programme for the first night of Thomas's travelogue, 14 August 1919. RIGHT An enthusiastic report in *The Sphere* of Thomas's opening lecture.

ROYAL OPERA HOUSE,
COVENT GARDEN.

PROPRIETORS - THE GRAND OPERA SYNDICATE. LTD.

Commencing Thursday Evening, August 14th, and Nightly at 8.30.
Matinees Wednesday, Thursday and Saturday at 2.30.

PERCY BURTON

(by arrangement with the Grand Opera Syndicate)

presents

AMERICA'S TRIBUTE TO BRITISH VALOUR

IN THE PERSON OF

LOWELL THOMAS

in

His Illustrated Travelogue of the British Campaigns:

With Allenby in Palestine

including

THE CAPTURE OF JERUSALEM

and

THE LIBERATION OF HOLY ARABIA.

The motion pictures used in this travelogue were taken by Mr. Harry A. Chase and Captain Frank Hurley. Still photographs by Mr. Chase. Art work by Miss Augusta A. Heyder. Projection by Mr. Chase.

Business Manager (for Lowell Thomas and Percy Burton) W. T. Cunningham.

With authority from the Secretary of War and the Secretary of the Navy of the United States Government, Mr. Lowell Thomas, accompanied by Colonel W. C. Hayes and a staff of photographers, journeyed over sixty thousand miles gathering material for a series of travelogues. Mr. Lowell Thomas was attached to the Allied forces in Europe, Asia and Africa, and was with them from the Orkney Islands to the forbidden deserts of Holy Arabia, from New York to Jerusalem, from Rome to Khartoum, from Paris to Salonika, and from Cairo to Berlin. He was the first pilgrim to tour the Holy Land by airplane, and the first person to go into the holy land of the Mohammedans with a cinema camera. After the signing of the armistice he was the first to visit Kiel, Hamburg, Berlin and other parts of Germany, and bring back the pictorial story of the German Revolution.

By arrangement with Mr. Percy Burton, Mr. Thomas cancelled a number of his engagements in America in order to appear at Covent Garden Royal Opera House for a limited period, under the auspices of the English-Speaking Union.

His travelogue on Allenby's crusade in Palestine and the liberation of Holy Arabia, is not a tale of Jules Verne, but the story of the reality of the present, surpassing the dreams of the imagination of the p

2^d

(*Under the auspices of* THE ENGLISH-SPEAKING UNION.)

President : Rt. Hon. A. J. BALFOUR, O.M.
Hon. President : The AMERICAN AMBASSADOR to England.
Vice-Presidents :

Field-Marshal Sir DOUGLAS HAIG, O.M.	Rt. Hon. J. R. CLYNES, M.P.
Rt. Hon. WINSTON CHURCHILL, M.P.	The ARCHBISHOP of CANTERBURY.
Earl CURZON of KEDLESTON, O.M.	BISHOP of LONDON, K.C.V.O.
The ARCHBISHOP of YORK.	Viscount BRYCE, O.M.
Sir ROBERT S. S. BADEN POWELL, K.C.B.	Earl of READING, G.C.B.
Rt. Hon. Sir ROBERT BORDEN, K.C.M.G.	Rt. Hon. W. M. HUGHES.
Viscount BURNHAM.	Viscount NORTHCLIFFE, &c.

WITH GENERAL ALLENBY at Covent Garden Theatre.

A Remarkable Film Lecture Telling the Strange Story of Colonel Thomas Lawrence, the Leader of the Arab Army

Colonel Thomas Lawrence (on Left) with Mr. Lowell Thomas

Colonel Lawrence is here seen at the entrance to his tent with Mr. Lowell Thomas, the American journalist, who at Covent Garden is telling the story of the Arab campaign

Colonel Thomas Lawrence

When war broke out Thomas Lawrence was a young archæological student engaged in work on ancient Mesopotamian cities. His knowledge of Arabia was first made use of in the map department at Cairo, and finally we find him as leader of the whole Arab Army in its fight from Mecca to Damascus. He wore this Arab style of dress throughout the campaign, and gained the confidence of chiefs and followers alike. A price was set upon his head but Colonel Lawrence won through to Damascus at the head of a devoted army

Copyrighted in the U.S.A.   *Drawn by D. Macpherson*

The Palestine Film Lecture at Covent Garden

"A large number of well-known personalities gathered on the opening night last week to hear Mr. Lowell Thomas's film lecture on the Palestine campaign. The lecturer showed pictures of Arab and other cavalry columns in motion which were quite unfamiliar to the man in the street

Mr. Lowell Thomas's wonderful pictures of the operations in Palestine, at Covent Garden, have revealed to many what a really big cavalry " show " means, and what it entails in the way of general organisation and detail, writes a military correspondent. Few laymen, at any rate in England, ever get the chance of seeing large bodies of cavalry massed for operations of war or of peace. In India, where there is elbow room and space, and where cavalry both on manœuvres and in the almost unending warfare on the N.-W. Frontier get more practice than any other cavalry in the world, we have, upon occasion, seen something of it. Ever since the times of what were called the " Kitchener tests," those of us who have served in India have had a taste of what the handling of large masses of Horse means. But even in India, when we perhaps had the equivalent of a cavalry division on manœuvres, it was a ceremonial parade compared to what this tremendous cavalry operation which Field-Marshal Lord Allenby conducted in Palestine connoted. These pictures, perhaps, brought home to the layman what it meant; they perhaps made him think of what it meant in terms of fodder, in terms of sore backs, and in terms of horse-shoes, quite apart from the little matter of the feeding and watering of both the horse and the man on his back. Good cavalry are supposed to be able to exist on the smell of an oil-rag; they are supposed to be able to fend for themselves if put to it.

Sometimes this thing is politely called " foraging," but people have also another name for it. Fending for yourself is possible when only a comparatively small body is involved; it is a different pair of shoes, however, when something very like a whole cavalry corps is on the warpath, as was the case in Palestine. Allenby started his service with the Inniskillings; he has been a cavalry soldier all his days, and the cavalry spirit has been breathed into him since the time when he first learnt how to " carry swords."

No one but a cavalry leader of such brilliance would have dared to conceive an operation of this magnitude over such country. Allenby, however, knew the quality of the cavalry he had under him—hunting yeomen from the " shires " and the " provinces." Anzacs who were bred in the saddle, Sikhs, Punjabis, Pathans, Gukkars from the Salt Range, natural horsemen, and, above all, horse-masters, every man Jack of them, and he took it on and knew that his Horse would not fail him. The most astounding fact to the cavalry soldier, who happens to know what it all meant, was the low percentage of casualties in horseflesh—on an all-round reckoning, less than 25 per cent. If the percentage had been 50 per cent. it would still have been a magnificent performance. As Mr. Lowell Thomas rightly adjudged, it is the most astonishing cavalry achievement in the whole history of war, ancient or modern.

the efforts of Winston Churchill, installed by Lloyd George in the Colonial Office and charged with the task of establishing order in a Middle East apparently careering towards catastrophe. In Egypt, for example, where Zaghlul Pasha, the founder of the nationalist Wafd party, had been exiled, rioting had led to the deaths of five Cairo students. In Palestine, the appointment of a Jew, Sir Herbert Samuel, as British High Commissioner, had enflamed the Arab population. In Irak, the British High Commissioner, Sir Percy Cox, had had to barricade himself into his residence. Churchill, in need of advisers, made Lawrence one of the most important.

In March 1921, Churchill called a conference at Cairo which was a little like a reunion of the Arab Bureau. Its first problem was that of Emir Abdullah, who had set out two months earlier at the head of a desperate column to drive the French from Damascus. In Transjordania, a largely unproductive area overlooked by the San Remo Conference, Kirkbride, once Lawrence's lieutenant, now the Commissioner, with only fifty men with which to resist this advance, had greeted the Emir with fulsome politeness. Sensibly, Abdullah had settled for the easily obtainable and proclaimed himself Emir of Transjordan. Equally amenable, the men in Cairo now endorsed this claim, on condition that Abdullah agreed to what he had already done and gave up his march on Damascus, and accepted what on the whole no longer concerned him, British suzerainty west of the Jordan. Unsurprisingly, Abdullah accepted these conditions.

This left Irak free in this game of musical thrones; it was offered to Feisal. (It is an indication of how cut-and-dried the Cairo decisions really were that the meeting at which Lord Winterton, of the Foreign Office, and Lawrence persuaded a bitter and reluctant Feisal to accept this crown was held three months before the conference convened!) There remained only one of the minor chores of imperialism; the single rival to Feisal was Sayed Talib, a leader in the pre-war secret society of nationalist Arab officers, Ahab. Leaving the High Commissioner's residence in Baghdad after a civilized tea, he suddenly found himself at gun-point, surrounded by khaki and clamped into an armoured car, this the brutal beginning of a journey which was to end in exile on the island of Ceylon. Left without serious opposition, Feisal was endorsed as king by a popular vote of 96·8 per cent; the will of the people having been heard, the British were piously happy to acquiesce in its verdict.

Hussein remained, rancorous and watchful, growling now at

the French, now at Ibn Saud, most of all at the British. It was decided to pay him off with a subsidy of £100,000 a year. (The same amount was paid to Ibn Saud to keep him from attacking Hussein – how simple imperialism was before oil complicated it!) In return, Hussein would be asked to accept all this 'disposal of the Arab countries' and the man chosen to do the asking was, oddly, Lawrence, whom Hussein had shown clearly enough in the past he neither liked nor trusted. This occasion was no different; the two men wrangled for week after week, the British using their control of the telegraphic offices to intercept, read and delay cables between Feisal and Hussein, Lawrence once going so far as to try to substitute an encouraging but mythical message from Zeid in order to keep Feisal calm. Hussein, however, remained obdurate and Lawrence left, this time to calm Abdullah, who was threatening resignation in Amman.

In Amman he remained for two months, acting as Chief British Representative, the appointment made by Churchill, who certainly hoped it would become permanent. But Lawrence, although he wrote in a footnote in *Seven Pillars of Wisdom* that Churchill had 'made straight all the tangle, finding solutions fulfilling (I think) our promises in letter and spirit (where humanly possible) . . .' and that therefore 'we were quit of the wartime Eastern adventure, with clean hands,' must, as his parentheses suggest, have had many reservations. Nor were the kingdoms of Arabia now those he had dreamed of, while his place in them, as just another British administrator, can only have seemed anomalous after the ambitions he had had. And, as he wrote in a foreword to the abridged *Seven Pillars of Wisdom,* he was under fire from Arab critics who did not share his view that Britain had worked her honour clear from the confusion. 'Like a tedious Pensioner I showed them my wounds (over sixty I have, each scar evidence of a pain incurred in Arab service) as proof I had worked sincerely on their side. They found me out-of-date: and I was happy to withdraw from a political milieu which had never been congenial.' Yet his withdrawal did not alter Hussein's curmudgeonly attitude and he refused every enticement to sign the proferred agreement until at last, in 1924, Ibn Saud swept him away into exile and so made his approval redundant. But meanwhile, Lawrence had wrenched himself clear of official affairs; as Churchill was to remark, 'He is a fine animal, but he cannot live in captivity.'

By 1922, he had already put together that vast, self-conscious aggregation of boast, confession, invective, humour, derring-do,

Lawrence's extensive experience among the Arabs fitted him for the post of adviser on Arab affairs.

ABOVE A group of some of the most influential figures in Middle Eastern affairs at this time. The photograph, taken at Amman in April 1921, includes Gertrude Bell (far left), Lawrence (centre), Sir Herbert Samuel (next to Lawrence) and Abdullah (next to Samuel).
RIGHT The Cairo Conference, which Churchill called in 1921. Churchill himself is fifth from the right in the first row, and Lawrence is fourth from the right in the second row.

207

insight and marvellous description, the work by which he hoped to justify his fame, a book sometimes dark as chiselled basalt, at others still volcanic and blood-red: *Seven Pillars of Wisdom*. It had come pouring from him; the manuscript mislaid or stolen on a journey, he had written it again, locked himself in with it, forced it from him, forced himself through the memory of the events it described, then, while in the Middle East at Churchill's behest, had trimmed its 400,000 words to near its present length. This, especially set and bound for him, he sent to such notable figures in the literary world as Bernard Shaw, Robert Graves and Edward Garnett. The trembling modesty of his covering letters disturbs one – if he felt like that, why did he bother such people with his work at all? 'Suddenly I remembered that your time was rubies. . . . Please don't, out of kindness, bore yourself.' These his protestations to Shaw, who quite properly ignored the book until persuaded by his wife's conviction that it was a masterpiece to sample it himself. Perhaps to his surprise, he found himself agreeing with her.

There is a grandeur about the book which no doubts can diminish. However unreliable or even dishonest it may be about Lawrence's military and political achievements, honesty remains its primary quality, a deep and troubling, implacable honesty which forces him to gaze directly at hardship, brutality, torture and betrayal, at his own agonized reaction to these, at the ambivalence within that agony, at his own betrayals of himself and those who trusted him and even at the lies with which he sometimes covered betrayal, ambivalence, agony and all. If it is too consciously grandiose, if the language is too mannered and seeks too obviously for the unexpected word, if detail sometimes covers everything with the relentlessness of a sand-dune, if even honesty occasionally falters and he turns away from some final revelation, nothing can lessen its majesty and force nor protect us from its thunderous impact.

What did it mean to Lawrence? It was of course the expression of his desperate desire to create some lasting work, to be an artist. More, it was a cleansing, a pouring out of memory, anguish and self-disgust, a vomiting up of all the dreadful and appalling experience of the previous three years, the convulsions of producing which almost destroyed him. But it was perhaps even more than that – a memorial to a lost love, as had been in some measure the whole Arabian adventure. 'To S.A.', the dedication proclaims, and the poem beneath it begins, 'I loved you, so I drew these tides of men into my hands . . .' and, later, says, 'Men prayed me that I set our work, the inviolate house, as a memory of you.' In a postscript he wrote, 'The strongest motive throughout had been a personal one, not mentioned here, but present to me, I think, every hour of these two years.' During the Peace Conference at Versailles he set out his reasons for involving himself in the Arab Revolt, his letter quoted by Knightley and Simpson in their *The Secret Lives of Lawrence of Arabia*; the motive he placed first was: 'Personal. I liked a particular Arab, and I thought that freedom for the race would be an acceptable present.'

There seems little doubt now that 's.a.' was Dahoum, that Salim Ahmed with whom Lawrence had been so uncomplicatedly happy in Carchemish. Nor is there any reason to doubt Knightley and Simpson when they quote Tom Beaumont, a machine-gunner who served with Lawrence (he is listed at the back of *Seven Pillars of Wisdom*); he told them that Dahoum was a Sherifiate spy, working behind the Turkish lines and sending news out to Lawrence by way of messengers. In September 1918 Lawrence left Umtaiye, outside Deraa, to return as arranged a few days later. Beaumont asked whether he had seen Salim. Lawrence replied: 'He's finished. He's dying. He's got typhoid.' And a little later, 'Lawrence turned away and pulled his *kuffieh* over his face and I heard him say "I loved that boy." When he turned back I could see that he had been weeping.' This story, if true, goes a long way to explain the strange mixture of ferocity and apartness which Lawrence felt during the advance from Deraa to Damascus. Nothing would have so exacerbated the guilty conflict within him as the death of the only person he loved in a cause which he knew himself to have betrayed from the beginning. Nothing would have made so bitter the anti-climax in Damascus, the long defeat of the post-war conferences, the sad shuffle of Feisal from throne to throne. And nothing could have made him feel more acutely the emptiness at the centre of the legend which had now gathered about his name.

It is not to be wondered at, therefore, if he now left that legend, as blinding yet insubstantial as a smoke-screen, to hold the attention of the world while he himself slipped further and further into the strange and half-resisted obscurity of the last phase of his life. As at the time of that mysterious hurt during his adolescence which had driven him into the Artillery, so now he went to ground in the anonymity of military life, this time in the RAF. He was perhaps influenced in this by his friendship with Lord

RIGHT Lawrence as a private
in the Tank Corps in 1924.
His quiet post in the
quartermaster's store,
dealing with army clothing,
left him time to pursue
his writing.

OPPOSITE Aircraftman Shaw
in 'scruff order', in India.

Trenchard, the founder and still commander of the service. He
nevertheless had difficulty in getting in; calling himself Ross, he
appeared at the recruiting office with false papers forged carelessly
enough to excite suspicion. Not even the higher authority he
could call on to get him over this hurdle (Trenchard had charged
his assistant, Air Vice-Marshal Sir Oliver Swann, with supervising
Lawrence's entry) persuaded the doctors to pass him; the recruiting officer, W. E. Johns, creator of the heroic *Biggles*, had to send
for an outside doctor in order to squeeze 'Ross' into the Air Force.
At first he had a difficult time, older than the other men, unused
to the martinets of the parade ground or the insanities of drill, not
supple enough to get through the physical training unhurt. So

210

211

badly did he feel he was being treated that Aldington has suggested he was being deliberately victimized by officers embarrassed at his anomalous presence, but it is more likely that his reaction to the ordinarily harsh discipline was more extreme and sensitive than that of his companions. A few months later, however, stationed at Farnborough and in the RAF School of Photography, he had become more contented.

At intervals he would appear in London, as quiet and contained and softly gregarious as ever, dealing with the problems of Edward Garnett's abridgment of *Seven Pillars of Wisdom* or soothing his lacerated spirit in the appreciation of such friends as Shaw and Graves. If he was a sort of *revenant*, shuttling between two worlds and somehow a ghost in both, he would not lie down in either. Petulantly, he would send his complaints about the RAF direct to Swann, to that officer's irritation. Soon everyone on the base knew who he was, so that it was small surprise when, on 27 December 1922, the *Daily Express* saw fit to hammer out headlines which also told the world outside. Trenchard offered him a commission as the only way to remain in the Service. Lawrence refused and, despite all his struggles, was once more a civilian by the end of January.

He needed, however, the props of organization, a structure which removed from him the unnecessary choices, gave him some element of regularity. He was in many ways adolescent all his life, undeveloped emotionally and sexually, and perhaps as a result craved the simple relationships and all-embracing discipline of a military establishment. Within that context, however, he needed something to occupy his mind, and what the services made available for that was machines. He delighted in aircraft, in the fact and the idea of them; now that they were barred to him, he turned to tanks. Thus, as T. E. Shaw, the name he would now bear for the rest of his life, he enlisted in the Tank Corps – using for the purpose his influence with one of Allenby's old commanders, Sir Philip Chetwode.

It was at this time that he first rented Clouds Hill, the small cottage, derelict then but set in order by him, in which he spent much of his free time. It stood not far from Bovington Camp in Dorset, where he was stationed, and it provided him with the gentler interludes he had to have in order to stand the easy-going brutalities of an army hut. And all this while, he was preparing the subscribers' edition of his enormous book, supervising the paper, the illustrations, the typography, the design, happily involved at

212

A drawing of Lawrence as Shaw in the RAF, by Augustus John, dated 1935.

last in the production of a book which would be an art-work in itself – a possibility which had excited him at intervals ever since his school days, and with which he had toyed many times.

Not only was he busy in these directions, he was at the same time carrying on a relentless campaign to get back into the RAF. He was not happy in the Army, certainly, but one senses that it was his dismissal he had to reverse; he had not, after all, been really happy in the RAF, either. The names of those he lobbied make a glittering array – Trenchard, naturally, Ramsay MacDonald, to no avail, Bernard Shaw, who wrote a curious letter to Baldwin, Churchill, John Buchan, who also wrote to Baldwin; to Edward Garnett he suggested that if he did not get his way he would

Clouds Hill Cottage

Here Lawrence occupied his leisure hours away from Bovington Camp and here he retired when he left the RAF in March 1935. The cottage represents various facets of his taste: the 'hall' decorated in the style of William Morris, teak doors brought back from Jiddah, a cryptic Greek motto from Herodotus over the door, and sleeping bags labelled 'Meum' and 'Tuum'.

BELOW The insulated room: in a glass case one of Lawrence's Arab robes is displayed, and on the wall hangs the insignia of his RAF squadron.
OPPOSITE, ABOVE The book room, which housed about 1,250 books. About half were contemporary works, and many were Hand Press books collected by Lawrence for their typography.
BELOW The music room. Lawrence had an impressive collection of records, many given to him by Charlotte Shaw.

commit suicide – 'I'm going to quit' – an adult tantrum which seems to have persuaded the authorities, themselves now harassed by an apparently endless stream of obdurate intellectuals, to place Lawrence where he wanted to be put.

In August 1925, Lawrence, or rather Shaw, as he still was, took his place once more in the RAF. And this time he and the life seem to have taken to each other. It is as though for the ten years he now served, something of the element which he had hoped to find did actually touch and calm him. But a new interest in what was increasingly the false Lawrence (as against the real T. E. Shaw) was about to arise – his subscribers' edition of *Seven Pillars of Wisdom*, and Garnett's abridgment, to be called *Revolt in the Desert*, were about to join Lowell Thomas's curious *With Lawrence in Arabia* on the bookshelves of the English-speaking world. Terrified that this new tide would overrun and drown him, he insisted on being transferred. Early in December 1926 he sailed for Karachi; in the England he had left, copies of his lovingly prepared edition, sold by him for £30 each, were being handed on for more than ten times that amount. (He gave Robert Graves a copy, knowing he was short of funds, and asked him to sell it, thus providing a poet's sustenance for the better part of a year.)

There passed calm months below the mountains of the North-West Frontier. Money was coming in, paying off at last the heavy costs of preparing and printing his book. He might have been modestly wealthy now; instead he diverted the flow of money to the RAF Memorial Fund. In fulfilment of a promise to show him anything he might write about the RAF, Lawrence had Edward Garnett show Trenchard the manuscript of *The Mint*, that garrulous and over-wrought work based on his experiences in the service. It was, he wrote, 'a worm's eye view of the RAF. . . . Any word used in barrack rooms has been judged good enough to go in . . .'; but he promised it would not be published before 1950, despite the fact that 'I would get £10,000 and a reputation as a writer' if it were. This voluntary censorship built up an inflated expectation for the book; when it did finally appear, in a world where people had learned new attitudes both to the services and to swearing, it caused little real excitement and added nothing to his reputation. In the meantime, however, Trenchard responded with an attack of dignified vapours.

Absurdity now catapulted Lawrence by chance into a kind of serenity. A wild and inaccurate report in the *Empire News* suggesting that he was stalking the mountains of Afghanistan dressed,

Two portraits of Lawrence
as Shaw, in RAF uniform:
ABOVE A painting by
William Roberts, now in
the Ashmolean.
BELOW An unfinished
portrait by Augustus John.

217

The British Schneider trophy team which in September 1931 gained the trophy permanently for Great Britain. They are shown gathered at Calshot Castle near where they were based. Lawrence was part of the team which helped to prepare the planes for this success. He also helped to test and design the motor launches later to be used in air-sea rescue operations.

or undressed, as a holy man and busily about the Secret Service's affairs, led to uproar in India, a flutter of inter-departmental cables, a would-be secret but sadly botched transfer home, questions in the House and yet another revival of interest in the Lawrence legend. One senses a popular feeling that all was well with the imperial fences as long as Lawrence was mending them. Furious, Lawrence resented all this, but it was his route to the RAF's new flying-boat station at the oddly named Cattewater, now less eccentrically Mount Batten.

So he came into his own. There were machines in plenty, for flying boats were popular, and he was one of those involved in the Schneider Trophy races. At the same time he had influence, for although the Minister for Air, Lord Thompson, warned him through Trenchard to have nothing whatsoever to do with the mighty of the land, Lawrence was not a man to take such prohibitions seriously. He had reforms in mind, and he knew the people who could help to push them through. As one direct result, the RAF's magnificent air/sea rescue service came into existence, to be the saviours of uncounted air-crews dropped by war into the

218

A photograph of Lawrence during his service with the RAF.

bleak hazards of the Channel. For most of the last four years of his service, he worked on refining the motor launches used, helping to produce in the end a swift and powerful boat quite different from the cumbersome vessel in which he had travelled to the sinking wreckage and the sodden corpses which had first focused his attention on the project.

It was near the end of February 1935 that Lawrence, now forty-seven, left the R A F. His face had lost its fierce angularity of nose and jaw, had become softer, almost puffy. The hair still lifted thickly above that jutting forehead, but no longer with the same electric energy. The clear eyes had dimmed a little, had receded into a small thicket of wrinkles. He had been somewhat afraid of this retirement; both giant and dwarf were roles he had played out. He talked sometimes of the grand posts he had been offered and might still take up, but these were the last wisps of distant dreams. Instead, he faced the chance of pointlessness, of losing direction, and a slow death at the finish: 'Nature would be merciful if she would end us at a climax and not in the decline,' he wrote to Nancy Astor. His old mentor Hogarth had died,

Trenchard was no longer head of the RAF he had created, Allenby now used his guile on fish: his fathers were passing relentlessly into oblivion.

Of all the friendships he had, there were perhaps two which had most sustained him in the years since self-disgust had made fame so discreditable. In Bernard Shaw's wife, Charlotte, he had found the warm, intelligent, concerned woman who could stand at last in place of his grim and toughly righteous mother. She was a decided woman who had suffered under the regime of her own mother and who as a result had forbidden herself to have children. She was warm, however, she found some quality in Lawrence which deeply engaged her and he responded to her interest with a constant honesty and, in his letters, an unusual directness of style. That he should have chosen and stuck to the name 'Shaw' may not have been the coincidence he always insisted it was.

The other relationship was very different; its existence unsuspected by almost everyone who knew him, it reveals another and secret, although not unexpected, dimension to his character. Involved this time was a man, a young Scot named John Bruce, and in *The Secret Lives of Lawrence of Arabia* he recounts, and Knightley and Simpson set down, the full story of his friendship with Lawrence. It is clear that Bruce felt great loyalty to this older man, made glamorous by fame, and that Lawrence was at ease with him, often told him his most private thoughts, turned to him when he wanted to expound the full measure of his despair and disappointment. When Lawrence joined the Army, Bruce joined with him, acting then as a sort of bodyguard and keeping Lawrence from the worst excesses of bullying and casual brutality. But that was not the limit of his functions. At intervals throughout those years, from 1923 until 1935, Lawrence, under what was surely the pretext of placating an aged relative, would ask Bruce to beat him. These seem to have been strange, antiseptic occasions, with nothing overtly sexual about them. The emphasis is somehow on Lawrence's endurance – 'He just lay there and gritted his teeth. He never moved. He was as tough as a rail.' Yet they were clearly compulsive events for Lawrence, masochistic rituals during which nerves perhaps shredded at Deraa could carry again lascivious echoes of that dreadful, exquisite pain. At the same time these meetings were banal, almost grotesque, the humiliation meaningless; learned by rote, such punishment could alleviate neither guilt nor desire.

Who was the Old Man at whose behest, so Lawrence insisted,

Lady Astor addressing a group of children during the Plymouth election, November 1923. Nancy Astor, MP for Plymouth, was one of the friends he made when stationed at Cattewater, and through her he was introduced to many of the stimulating people from the world of politics and the arts who visited her at home.

An aerial pageant at Hendon, July 1920. Lord Trenchard (second from the left), the founder of the RAF, was consistently against Lawrence joining the force.

these thrashings were administered? What figure of faceless, indefinable authority did he represent if he was, as he must have been, created from Lawrence's fantasy? Was he that missing parent, the firm-willed father, whose strength might at last set bounds on the hard will of the mother? Was he the externalized form of the feelings Lawrence expressed in 1923 in a letter to the publisher Lionel Curtis?:

We are all guilty alike, you know. You wouldn't exist, I wouldn't exist, without this carnality. Everything with flesh in its mixture is the achievement of a moment when the lusty thought of Hut 12 has passed into action and conceived: and isn't it true that the fault of birth rests somewhat on the child? I believe it's we who led our parents on to bear us, and it's our unborn children who make our flesh itch. A filthy business all of it. . . .

Or was Lawrence expiating only his later guilts, his betrayal of the Arabs who had been his comrades, of the Arab whom he had loved?

In any case, there his life had been, poised for a decade between the secret compulsions of pain and the soothing affection of

221

Lawrence on his Brough motor-cycle at Clouds Hill. He once confessed to Liddell Hart: 'Speed is the second oldest animal craving in our nature.'

Charlotte Shaw. Settled between these poles, stabilized by the military order about him, he had changed. Some truculent assertion, some madness of ambition, the desire to be seen, to be known, to be acknowledged, the passion to act, to exercise the will – all the springs of action which had moved him through his first thirty years – had now run down. He felt, as he wrote to Lady Astor, that there was 'something broken in the works'. In April, he wrote to a friend that he was 'very empty in mind, tired-out and futile-feeling'. To his old friend the artist Eric Kennington, he wrote early in May, 'Days seem to dawn, suns to shine, evenings to follow, and then I sleep. What I have done, what I am doing, what I am going to do, puzzle me and bewilder me. Have you ever been a leaf and fallen from your tree in autumn and been really puzzled about it? That's the feeling.'

On 13 May winter gathered in what autumn had marred. Lawrence rode his motor-cycle, his big Brough Special, to Bovington Camp to cable a friend an invitation to lunch. On the way back to Clouds Hill he pulled in to make room for a black van. As he

222

came over a rise, he saw immediately in front of him two errand-boys on cycles. He swerved abruptly. The motor-cycle fell away, its engine roaring. Tumbling, it corkscrewed onwards down the road, Lawrence already flung aside. His head broke open, blood masked him, his dreams dwindled into coma. Six days later, he died.

At his funeral, all his worlds gathered; those who had known only Lawrence of Arabia mingled with those who had known only Aircraftman Shaw. The writers and artists, the politicians and administrators, the officers and men, came together like ambassadors from distant countries in all of which Lawrence had been a notable citizen. Yet the one representative he might have wished most of all to be there was not present. No one was sent by the Chapman family.

Eric Kennington's effigy of Lawrence, his camel-whip on his right.

Further Reading

Aldington, Richard, *Lawrence of Arabia: A Biographical Enquiry* (Collins, 1955).

Antonius, George, *The Arab Awakening* (Hamish Hamilton, 1938).

Armitage, Flora, *The Desert and the Stars* (Faber, 1956).

Benoist-Méchin, *Lawrence d'Arabie ou le Rêve Fracassé* (Clairefontaine, Lausanne, 1961).

Knightley, Philip, and Simpson, Colin, *The Secret Lives of Lawrence of Arabia* (Nelson, 1969).

Lawrence, A. W. (ed.), *T. E. Lawrence by his Friends* (Jonathan Cape, 1937).

Lawrence, A. W. (ed.), *Letters to T. E. Lawrence* (Jonathan Cape, 1962).

Nutting, Anthony, *Lawrence of Arabia: The Man – and the Motive* (Hollis & Carter, 1961).

Villars, Jean Béraud-, *T. E. Lawrence: or the Search for the Absolute* (Sidgwick & Jackson, 1958).

In the years between the wars there were a number of largely hagiographic biographies, notably *With Lawrence in Arabia* by Lowell Thomas, published by Hutchinson in 1924, Robert Graves's *Lawrence and the Arabs*, published by Jonathan Cape in 1927, and *T. E. Lawrence: In Arabia and After* by Liddell Hart, also published by Jonathan Cape, in 1934.

There are, finally, the books and letters written by T. E. Lawrence himself, notably the following:

Seven Pillars of Wisdom (Jonathan Cape, 1935; Penguin Books, 1962).

The Mint (Doubleday, New York, 1935; Jonathan Cape, 1955).

Letters to his Biographers (Cassell, 1963).

The Letters of T. E. Lawrence (ed. David Garnett) (Jonathan Cape, 1938).

The Home Letters of T. E. Lawrence and his Brothers (Blackwell, 1954).

List of Illustrations

Picture research by Pat Hodgson.

The maps on pages 108 and 109 were drawn by Edward McAndrew Purcell.

Index

230